PRAYER WORKS!
40 DAYS & 40 NIGHTS VIOLENT PRAYERS AGAINST TOUGH PROBLEMS

BECOMING VIOLENT WHEN THE SITUATION GET TOUGH
800 ATOMIC BOMB PRAYERS
40 THUNDER QUOTES
BEST APPLICATION FOR FASTING AND PRAYER

Copyright © 2017 By:
OLUSEGUN FESTUS REMILEKUN
Fessy Ventures Limited
pastorfessy@yahoo.co.uk
All scriptures quotations are from the King James Version of the Bible.
Copy Right © Pastor Fessy 2017

All Rights reserved, No part of this publication may be reproduced or transmitted in any form or by any means, electronic or mechanical, including photocopy, recording or any information storage and retrieval system, without permission in writing from the copyright owner.

Publisher: Olusegun Festus Remilekun
For more information prayers and counseling

Contact:
Pastor Olusegun Festus Remilekun (Pastor Fessy)
Tel: +2348039402644 OR +2348079877604
Email: pastorfessy@yahoo.co.uk
pastorfessy@gmail.com

DEDICATION

This prayer book is dedicated to the GOD OF SIGNS AND WONDERS that compensated us with twins; signs and wonders.

May your name continue to reign from everlasting to everlasting.

TABLE OF CONTENTS

Dedication

Table of Contents

Acknowledgment

Preface

Day One: Rebuild your Faulty Foundation

Day Two: Beware of your Enemy

Day Three: Pulling Down the Altar against your Destiny

Day Four: My Enemies must Die Mysteriously

Day Five: Reversing the Curse in your Life to Blessing

Day Six: War against Unfriendly Friends and Household Enemies

Day Seven: Breaking the Satanic Yoke upon your Life

Day Eight: Fortify Yourself against Blood Sucker

Day Nine: Divine Reinforcement against Satanic Agents

Day Ten: Wake Up From Your Slumber

Day Eleven: Freedom from Satanic Prison

Day Twelve: Recharge and be in charge

Day Thirteen: How Old is your Problem

Day Fourteen: Set that Evil Garment Ablaze

Day Fifteen: Leave that Curse Land

Day Sixteen: Only the Violent can take it by Force

Day Seventeen: No Retreat, No Surrender

Day Eighteen: Liberated from the Power of Poverty

Day Nineteen:	Confronting that Mountain with your faith
Day Twenty:	Poverty Must Leave My Life
Day Twenty-One:	Pray your Way out of that Problem
Day Twenty-Two:	Contacting the Anointing to Produce Result
Day Twenty-Three:	Move Forward, Don't move Backward
Day Twenty-Four:	Pay the Price and be Great
Day Twenty-Five:	Open your Door with the Key of Prayer
Day Twenty-Six:	Breaking Record with your Gift to Provoke Heaven
Day Twenty-Seven:	Enlarge my Coast
Day Twenty-Eight:	It is my Set time of Settlement
Day Twenty-Nine:	Work Hard Before it gets Hard
Day Thirty:	Pursue, Overtakes and Recover All
Day Thirty-One:	Don't give Up, help is on the Way
Day Thirty-Two:	Authorized to be Fruitful
Day Thirty-Three:	Remember Me Oh Lord
Day Thirty-Four:	Open my Eyes Oh Lord
Day Thirty-Five:	Marked for Promotion
Day Thirty-Six:	It is my Turn to Laugh
Day Thirty-Seven:	The Present Helper in the Time of Needs
Day Thirty-Eight:	I will not Labor in Vain
Day Thirty-Nine:	Open A New Chapter in my Life
Day Forty:	Balance Your Miracle with Thanksgiving

ACKNOWLEDGMENT

- God the Father, God the Son and God the Holy Spirit, thanks for rescuing me from the hand of the devil, and a very BIG thanks, for inspiring, guiding, leading, and teaching me how to write this book.

- Pastor Taiwo Ajayi: My mentor, spiritual father, and counselor, a man that always leaves a good legacy. May the oil upon you never run dry in Jesus name.

- My Wife Grace: You are a gift sent from above to me because you are always there playing my role when I am not around so that the children won't feel my absent. You are a woman worthy to be praised.

PREFACE

PRAYER WORKS is forty days and forty nights prayer plan, specially prepared for your spiritual explosion and breakthroughs in life. These are special Holy days set aside to seek the face of God over a particular issue. It is a period to reason with God one on one, a set time one need to go solo with His maker when things get though and one need divine intervention. It could be relating to God things you can't relate with your fellow human.

A time to fellowship with the Almighty God alone without distractions, a time to empty all your problems on the throne of grace. I have no doubts, that after this forty days and forty nights encounter with God, there will be a divine solution concerning that problem that has stayed long in your life and is resisting solution in Jesus name. It is also a moment of travail and wrestles to get what belongs to you back. During this period, you need a pen and a book because God will give you information, revelation, and inspiration.

After Moses spent 40 days and 40 nights in the presence of the LORD in Exodus 34:27-28, the Bible says "And the LORD said unto Moses Write thou these words: for after the tenor of these words I have a covenant with thee and with Israel. And he was there with the LORD forty days and forty nights; he did neither eat bread nor drink water. And he wrote upon the tables the words of the covenant the Ten Commandments." Ideas rule the world, if you are not informed, you will be deformed. I speak life into your brain, receive ideas to become productive in life. After this forty days and forty night experience, God will give you a marketable idea to make money, in Jesus name.

A short pen is better than a long memory, please write down anything you receive in form of information, remember what Habakkuk 2:2-3 says "And the LORD answered me, and said, write the vision and make it plain upon tables, that he may run that readeth it. For the vision is yet for an appointed time, but at the end, it shall speak, and not lie: though it tarry, wait for it, because it will surely come, it will not tarry" Please note, you must be in the Spirit, with your spiritual antenna on. Moses had to write down the vision for his mission.

After God destroyed the first world with flood in Genesis 7, in verse 17, the Bible says "And the flood was forty days upon the earth; and the waters increased, and bare up the ark, and it was lifted up above the earth" May God lift you up above the earth, in Jesus name. In Genesis 8:6 "And it came to pass at the end of forty days, that Noah opened the window of the ark which he had made" Window is very important in a house because of ventilation. For someone reading this book, you will experience open heaven and God will open the windows of heaven upon you and release uncommon blessings upon your life, in Jesus name. That unpleasant situation in any area of your life will become pleasant in Jesus name.

1Kings 18:4, Jezebel killed some Prophets of God, and Obadiah hid a hundred Prophets in two different caves. Elijah became wanted by Ahab, he later confronted Ahab one on one, that he is the only Prophet of the LORD left but Baal has four hundred and fifty Prophets, 450 Prophets of Baal contested against Elijah in a match, Elijah killed all of them and their head Jezebel heard and she became angry that under 24 hours she is going to kill Elijah. The moment Elijah heard that Jezebel was after his life, he ran for his life to a particular place with his servant. He left his servant and went a day journey into the desert because he was afraid and frustrated. He decided to give up and prayed that God should take his life, not too long he slept off. The angel of God woke him up, fed him the first time, he slept, woke him up the second time, and told him to eat because the journey before him is too great. He ate and traveled in the strength of the food he ate for forty days and forty nights unto mount Horeb. Elijah acted in a coward way when he heard that Jezebel was after his life because he has just finishing killing four hundred and fifty Prophets of Baal and has not recharged to face their head, Jezebel

The angelic food he ate empowered him. After Elijah has recharge fully, he became bold and prophesy how Jezebel, the strong woman after his life will die according to 1 Kings 21:23 "And of Jezebel also spake the LORD saying, the dogs shall eat Jezebel by the wall of Jezreel." In II Kings 9:32-26, Jezebel died mysteriously, she was thrown down, from a story building, dogs came and ate her flesh, and drank her blood and during her funeral, it was her skeleton that was buried. I decree a mysterious death upon anyone after you life today, in Jesus name.

In Luke 4:1-14, Our Lord Jesus Christ discovered the importance of forty days and 40 nights, before he commenced his ministry. He spent his own forty days and forty nights in the wilderness, a wild region that is very difficult to live. He moved to the next level to face the devil because for every next level, there is a next devil to face. Jesus defeated the devil flat with the word, and in verse 14, the Bible says "And Jesus returned in the power of the spirit into Galilee and there went out a fame of him through the entire region about him." I pray for you reading this book, after this spiritual exercise, in the name that is above every other name, you will become famous to the world, a terror to principalities and power and a topic to the entire world, in Jesus name. These prayers will work for you, in Jesus mighty name!

Olusegun F. Remilekun

DAY ONE

REBUILD YOUR FAULTY FOUNDATION

Text: Judges 11: 1-3

Thunder Quote: (Your future is bigger than where you were born.)

The Foundation of anything in life is very important because Foundation determine the destiny of anything. So many Christians Foundation is responsible for their problem. In Psalm 11:3 the Bible says, "If the foundation be destroyed, what can the righteous do? The foundation is in plural form, it could be marital foundation, academicals foundation, family foundation or ministerial foundation. So many people are suffering today because of bad foundation laid by their forefather's and parents.

Foundation is what something is built upon. If the foundation of a three story building is not solid, the three story building will collapsed after some period of time. Many houses collapsed due to bad foundation and sub-standard building materials used. Don't ever build on your forefather's foundation or your father's foundation if you discover their foundation is faulty. The place we read in Psalm 11: 3 says, what can the righteous do? You can be born again; spirit filled and still be affected with generational curse, if your foundation is faulty. For instance, if your parents are idol worshipper, and they named you according to the name of their idol. You must change that name if you desire a change. If the foundation of your family is built upon the devil, it will affect your destiny.

In Judges 6, Gideon was having a foundational problem because of the altar of Baal in his father's house. If you build the foundation of your life on the faulty foundation of your father, you will end where your father ended and also achieve the same result with your father, at the end, people will mock you by saying, like father like son. It is a pity today; many of us are reaping the bad seed sowed by our ancestors. The law of harvest in Galatians 6: 7, which ought to work in our favor is working against us. Foundation is what makes life meaningful. When your foundation is build on the Rock of Ages (Jesus) your destiny will be secured and guaranteed.

In our Bible text, Jephthah's mother was a harlot and his step brothers mocked him that he can't have inheritance in their father's house because he is a son of a strange woman, he ran from his brethren to another land. The bad foundation of his mother being a harlot made him to run away. What is that reproach in your life that has ridiculed you among your mate? May the Almighty God roll it away now, in Jesus name. 1Corinthians 3: 11 says. "For other foundation can no man lay that is laid, which is Jesus Christ." If you desire a bright future or you want to live heaven on earth, make sure your life is cemented on the Rock of Ages (Jesus Christ). It is either you build on Christ or the devil. A song says "On Christ the Solid Rock I stand, all other ground is sinking sand." Your future is bigger than where you were born; don't allow anything to stand as an obstacle to your destiny. If you need to go extra mile spiritually so that your foundation can be corrected, be bold, and do it fast.

The only one that can build your future life to have meaning when you make him your foundation is Jesus. In Psalm 127: 1a, the Bible says, "Except the LORD build the house, they labor in vain that build it." I pray concerning that uncompleted project in your life, may the Almighty God take charge, and complete it for you, in Jesus name. It is only the foundation of God that is standard sure- 11Timothy 2: 19.

HOW CAN I REBUILD MY FAULTY FOUNDATION

(1) Demolish the old faulty foundation -Matthew 15: 13.
(2) Hand over the new foundation to God -Psalm 127: 1a.
(3) Use standard materials like:
   I. The word of God Hebrew- 4: 12.
   II. Faith Hebrew -11: 1, 6.
   III. The blood of Jesus Revelation- 12: 11
   IV. The anointing Isaiah -10: 27.
   V. Fasting.
   VI. Prayer.
   VII. Praise.

PRAYER BOMB

1. Father Lord, I thank you for repairing the fault, affecting the foundation of my life, in Jesus name.
2. Father Lord, every sin committed by my forefather's that is affecting my destiny, please have mercy, in Jesus name.
3. Blood of Jesus, wash away every atrocity and evil deed I have done, in the past in Jesus name.
4. Father Lord, don't let me end where my father ended, in Jesus name.
5. Father Lord, let my new arrival as a believer; into my family bring a change to my family, in Jesus name.

6. Father Lord, don't let my past affect my future, in Jesus name.
7. My Father, my maker, let every evil sacrifice offered upon the foundation of my family; receive fire, in Jesus name.
8. Father Lord, I build every foundation of my life on Jesus Christ the Rock of Ages.
9. My Father, my maker, let every satanic Foundation constructed against my life, collapse by fire, in Jesus name.
10. Father Lord, every evil declaration upon my destiny, I cancel it with the blood of Jesus.
11. My Father my maker, I command every evil spirit chasing me out of my home, to leave my life, in Jesus name.
12. Father Lord, let every idol or image planted on the foundation of my life, be uprooted and catch fire, in Jesus name.
13. Father Lord, let every star hunter and dream killer against my life, die by fire, in Jesus name.
14. Father Lord, let every gang up demons against my family, business, and marriage, scatter by fire, in Jesus name.
15. Every spirit of go-slow operating in my life, get out by fire and locate your sender, in Jesus name.
16. Father, let every witches and wizard manipulating my destiny anywhere, die by fire, in Jesus name.
17. Every power from my father's house hindering my progress in life, receive fire, in Jesus name.
18. Father, loose and set me free from every curse following me from birth, in Jesus name.
19. My Father my maker, let anybody using evil power to cover my glory from shining, die by fire, in Jesus name.
20. Father, I pull down and set ablaze, any evil altar and shrine working, against my destiny in my father's house, in Jesus name.

DAY TWO

BEWARE OF YOUR ENEMY

Text: Job 1:6 -12

Thunder Quote: (You must be wise as the serpent to rebuke the old serpent the devil.)

Job was a successful business man until the devil launch attack against his business and his business collapsed. Satan has strategies he uses in attacking people's destiny. He operates from the four corners of the earth; east, west, north, and south. His three fold mission is to steal, kill and destroy according to the book of John 10:10a. The Bible advised us in 1Peter 5:8, to sober, vigilant because our enemy the devil, as a roaring lion, walketh about, seeking for whom he may devour.

BEWARE from Oxford Advance Learner's Dictionary means, warning that something or somebody is dangerous and that one should be careful. It also means to be cautious, vigilant and alert to detect danger. For you to be able to detect signs that enemy is around, your spiritual antenna must be always at work to give you signal. You must be wise as a serpent to rebuke the old serpent, the devil. The enemy, on the other hand, means someone who opposes or seeks to inflict injury on another individual. In nut a shell, the enemy is anything that harms something or prevents it from being successful. The enemy is a constant force in a man's life. Everything God created has an enemy. Every living thing is operating under the atmosphere of the enemy in the world. We are in the world, but not of the world, because the god of this world is the devil. Life is full of enemies; the enemy of a rat is a cat, the enemy of chicks is a hawk, the enemy of insects is birds, the enemy of Christian is the devil and the enemy of the spirit is the flesh. An adage says, the devil you know is better than the angel you don't know. In one of our course in the school of disciples, we were thought, know your enemy. When God reveals your enemy to you, it will be impossible for the enemy to kill you. 11 Corinthians 2:11 says, "Less Satan should get an advantage of us; for we are not ignorant of his devices." Ignorant is a killer.

7 DANGEROUS AND DEADLY ENEMIES TO BEWARE OF

(1) Disobedience: It with hold God's blessing and rain curses upon someone. It brings natural consequences of our action. Lot's wife looked back and became a pillar of salt, Jonah disobeyed God and ended up in the belly of fish, King Saul disobeyed God and lost his kingship position, Ananias and his wife died mysteriously due to disobedience.

(2) Sin: Sin and disobedience are similar, but sin is more dangerous because it's total rebellion against the known will of God. You can't become who God created you to be if you persist in rebelling against God, destroying your relationship with God through sin is suicide.

(3) Fear: Fear is having faith in the impossible. Someone said, it is False Evidence Appearing Real. He who fears to try will never know what he could have done. He who fears God has nothing to fear. God has not given us the spirit of fear, 11 Tim. 1:7.

(4) Discouragement: Discouragement has truncated many people's destinies, dreams, and potentials in our generation.

God will not give you a dream unless he knows you have the ability and capability to complete it. Do what needs to be done no matter how difficult or impossible God commands feel.

(5) Procrastination: If you wait for a perfect condition, you will never get anything done. Procrastination often grows out of discouragement. When we become discouraged, we stop finding a reason for doing what we know we can do. One of the cures for procrastination is eliminating all excuses and reason for not taking action.

(6) Distractions: Satan uses distraction to stop our progress in life or at least, to change the speed of our progress. Never sacrifice the right thing for the good things. Anything that doesn't help our progress hinders it. If a plan or an activity distract you from accomplishing your vision according to God's schedule, it is bad for you at that moment.

(7) Past Failure: We are unwilling to take a risk in the presence because we have failed in the past. Failure is never a reason to stop trying. It is better to try and fail than never to try at all.

If you don't forget your past failure, it will affect your future success. One of the things that helped the career of Paul was, he forget his past mistakes according to Philippians 3:13b, Paul says, "but this one thing I do forgetting those things which are behind and reaching forth unto things which are before."

PRAYER BOMB

(1) Father, thank you for revealing every plan of the enemy to me, in Jesus name.

(2) Father, paralyzed by fire every enemy saying NO to my progress, in life Jesus name.

(3) Father, place an hedge of protection round about me, in Jesus name.

(4) Father, defend your name in my life as the Lord of Host, in Jesus name.

(5) Father, let every territorial strongman behind the problem affecting my life, somersault and die, in Jesus name.

(6) Father, let my glory that the enemy has buried, come out by fire, in Jesus name.

(7) My Father Lord, let every BUT in my life that has ridiculed me, receive fire, in Jesus name.

(8) Every stranger hiding in my life, fall down and die, in Jesus name.

(9) Father, let your consuming fire go ahead of me and consume every enemy waiting for me, in the future in Jesus name.

(10) Father, I secure and insure everything that belongs to me with the blood of Jesus against any lost, in Jesus name.

(11) Father, let every satanic map, calabash, mirror or garget the enemy is using to monitor my life, scatter by fire, in Jesus name.

(12) Holy Ghost fire, burn by fire, every satanic property the enemy has deposited in my life, in Jesus name.

(13) Every satanic attachment in my life, be separated by fire, in Jesus name.

(14) Father Lord, give me rapid promotion in my entire endeavor this month, in Jesus name.

(15) Every arrow of disaster fired against me, miss your target and locate your sender, in Jesus name.

(16) Father Lord, please let me enjoy the benefit of all my labor, in Jesus name.

(17) My Father my maker, give me an amazing miracle, which will surprise every household enemy that want to see my downfall, in the name of Jesus.

(18) Father, let every era of slavery in my life, end today, in Jesus name.

(19) Father, lift me up out of every pit of rise and fall hindering my progress, in life in Jesus name.

(20) Father, give me wisdom to be able to discern every trick of the devil, in Jesus name.

DAY THREE

PULLING DOWN THE ALTAR AGAINST YOUR DESTINY

Text: Judges 6: 23-31

Thunder Quote: (Don't allow your family background to put on the ground.)

In respect of our Bible text, God proved himself to Gideon as Jehovah Shalom (The LORD of Peace). Gideon decided to build an altar for God in appreciation. That same night, God told him to throw down the evil altar of Baal in his father's house, because God is a jealous God, you can't serve him and also have another god. In Exodus 20: 3-5 the Bible says, "Thou shalt have no other god before me. Thou shalt not bow down thyself to them, nor serve them: for I the LORD thy God am a jealous God, visiting the inquiring of the fathers upon the children unto the third fourth generation of them that hate me." You can't serve two gods, you must choose one.

The father of Gideon was a worshipper of Baal when he was still alive. The altar he constructed before he died became a barrier against the progress of his son. I pray for a user of this book, every altar erected by your forefathers that is affecting your life is destroyed, in Jesus name. Baal is a male god of the Phoenicians and Canaanites is a counterpart of the female Ashtaroth, connected with immorality. Unless you destroy the altar in your father's house, you are not a free man. Altar in Three-in-one Bible reference companion means, a raised structure or place on which sacrifice are offered or incense is burned in worship.

I don't know the altar in your village or in your father's house receiving sacrifice on your behalf, may the fire if God from heaven come upon the altar now and dismantle it now, in Jesus name. The foundation of Gideon was faulty because of the evil altar his father constructed. Psalm 11:3 says, "If the foundation be destroyed, what can the righteous do?" A lot of problem facing people today are as a result of bad satanic bondage due to their family background. Don't allow your family background to put you on the ground. If your father serves the god of iron, the god of thunder, or oracle, must you answer the name of their gods? The name you answer matters a lot. Satanic names are affecting so many Christian's destiny. When I was in the Secondary School, there was a particular student we used to call dead-man; he liked the evil name because he didn't stop anyone from calling him the name.

Unfortunately, before he finished Secondary School, he fell sick and died. What you accept into your life will manifest in your life. Dead-man would have been alive if had changed his name to living-man. Do you know the meaning of your name? during Secondary School days also, due to ignorance, one of my friends was being called KASETA, meaning Lord of madness, the name affected him, to extend he was always in an uncompleted house in the bush, smoking Indian hemp, drinking alcohol and violating the school laws. He was also given an award on paper as the most notorious in my school in 1988. Proverbs 22: 1 says, "A good name is rather to be chosen than great riches, and loving favor rather than silver and gold." May the name of Jesus cancel every evil name affecting your life, in Jesus name. In most villages in African today, altars are so common everywhere. I visited a particular family in Ojo, Lagos State, and the Holy Spirit opened my eyes, and I discovered that in their sitting room an altar was constructed, also in their neighborhood. The altar of the god of iron is so common, their worshippers will always offer sacrifices on their altar, pouring blood, oil and other things to appease their god. A pastor friend told me this story; the He said there was a particular idol in my father's house in the village, it has some forbidden things you must not eat or else a strange sickness will come upon you. My father disobeyed and ate what the idol forbid unknowingly, and a strange sickness came upon him. He went to make inquiry and it was revealed to him that he ate what the idol in his father's house forbid, he confronted the idol and said, "look at what you have brought upon my body, today mark an end of serving you." That was over 15years, he is still alive because he now knows Jesus. What you believe in matters a lot, as a man thinketh in his heart, so is, Proverb23:7.

An altar is a place where the wicked people make evil enchantment and incantation against people destiny, so many businesses, marriage, families, and finances are being tied to satanic altars to cover their glory from shining. Also, when they want to kill anyone, they will go to their altar, make enchantment, call the person's name and that is the end of that person. I pray for you, in the name that is above every other name, anyone mentioning your name or the names of your family members in any altar for evil, may the fire of God fall upon them from heaven, and consume them, in Jesus name.

PRAYER BOMB

(1) Father, I thank you for destroying every altar erected against my destiny, in Jesus name.

(2) Father, let every altar receiving blood, animals, oil and anything on my behalf to exist, receive fire and scatter by fire, in Jesus name.

(3) Father, let every evil covenant, oath or agreement anyone has entered with the devil on my behalf, break in Jesus name.

(4) Holy Ghost fire, the blood of Jesus, visit and repair the foundation of my family, in Jesus name.

(5) Any tongue saying negative things or evil prophesy into my destiny, I cut you off in Jesus name.

(6) God of Elijah, arise by fire and visit the root and the source of my problem by fire, in Jesus name

(7) Father, every evil name from the pit of hell attached to my life, I delete it with the name of Jesus.

(8) Father Lord, every ritual my ancestors or parents have made on any altar against my destiny, I cancel it with the blood of Jesus.

(9) Father, let every strange god worshipped by my forefather's claiming ownership of me, received fire and leave me alone, in Jesus name.

(10) Every crying blood against my life, I silent you with the blood of Jesus.

(11) Anyone or anybody mentioning my name in any altar or shrine to kill me, receive fire and die by fire, in Jesus name.

(12) Father, any food offered to any idol that I have eaten knowingly or unknowingly, that is working against me, I neutralize it, in Jesus name.

(13) Any idol or image anywhere representing me in any shrine, receive fire and burn by fire.

(14) Every ancient curse that affected my forefather's and is repeating itself in my time break, in the name of Jesus.

(15) My glory, my star, my destiny receive fire from heaven and shine, in Jesus name.

(16) Father, every satanic festival I have participated in, that is standing against my progress, I renounce it now, in Jesus name

(17) Father, let any village power from my village working against me, receive fire from heaven and be powerless, in Jesus name.

(18) God of Elijah, release the fire of death upon every satanic priest assigned by my enemy to kill me, in Jesus name.

(19) Father, release the fresh fire of revival upon my prayer altar, in Jesus name.

(20) My Father my maker, let every evil ancient altar in my father's house, catch fire and collapse, in Jesus name.

DAY FOUR

MY ENEMIES MUST DIE MYSTERIOUSLY

Text: Numbers 16:1-5, 28-35

Thunder Quote: (Without a complete armour going into the battle field is suicide).

The world is a battle field; the battle begins from the first day one is born into the world. There are some enemies that have been existing before you came into this world, some of these enemies do not want you to come, they have tried there possible best ever since you were in the womb to truncate your destiny, thank God you are alive.

When you read Revelation 12:1-17, you will have a clear understanding. To survive in the battle of life, you must be ready to attack the enemy. The enemy is not a respecter of age; he is ready to kill anybody, whether young or old. If you don't want to die before your time, you must kill any enemy that wants you dead with your tongue. There is power in your tongue, according to Proverbs 18:21a, "Death and life are in the power of the tongue." You have the mandate to also decree death upon your enemies, because in Job 22:28b, the Bible says, "Thou shalt also decree a thing, and it shall be established unto thee." As a genuine child of God, you are a royal seed and a royal priesthood that rules by decree. From our text in Numbers 16:28-32, Korah, Dathan and Abiram challenge Moses and he decreed mysterious death upon them, the earth opened her mouth and swallowed them up. Please always remember, whenever you face the enemy that life and death are in your tongue because you are God's battle axe. In Psalm 120:7, Psalmist says, "I am for peace: but when I speak, they are for war." You are a dangerous weapon in the hand of God according to Isaiah 41:15 that says, "see, I will make thee a new sharp threshing instrument having teeth: thou shalt thresh the mountains, and beat them small, and shall make the hills as chaff."

Prayer is a powerful weapon that you can use to defeat the enemy. Prayer is like a bullet that comes out of the mouth of a believer. The Bible says, "pray without ceasing." 1 Thessalonians 5:17. As long as you are still alive, you are not immune from attack, it can occur anytime. When you pray fervently and violently, the death of your enemy will be mysterious. Mysterious from dictionary means, difficult to understand, or explain; strange. For instance, in 1Samuel 17, the death of Goliath was mysterious, imagine a little boy like David defeating Goliath a giant and a man of war from his youth, it is beyond human understanding, only God can make such happen. David used to sling on him, despite the spear, sword, and shield with him, the moment David slang Goliath's forehead with a stone, he fell down and was in a coma, David beheaded him quickly. When Goliath men discovered that he is dead, they fled all fled for their lives. I don't a know that Goliath troubling your life, family business, before sunset today, you will hear the announcement of his Obituary, in Jesus name!

The way Jezebel died in II Kings 9:31-37, in that order, every strong man or strong woman after your life, they will die mysteriously! Their bodies will be scattered everywhere, in a way that part of their bodies will be missing during their funeral, in Jesus name. Exodus 22:18 says, "Thou shall not suffer a witch to live." In order words, every witch or wizard must die." The Bible says, There is no peace, saith the Lord, unto the wicked-Isaiah 57:21. In Exodus Chapter fourteen, after the children of Israel were released from the land of bondage, in Egypt, the Egyptian pursue them, God set trap for the Egyptian, unknown to them by parting the sea, as the children of Israel were walking on the dry ground in the midst of the sea, the Egyptians followed them behind and Moses stretched out his hand over the sea, the Lord's trap caught all of them and they all perished in the sea. God will cause your enemies to make a silly mistake that will end their lives this month, in Jesus name. I don't know that man or woman that wants you dead by all means, tonight, they will all sleep the sleep of death, that will land them in the mortuary before sunrise tomorrow, in Jesus name.

Ephesians 6:12 says, "For we wrestle not against flesh and blood, but against principalities, against powers, against the rulers of the darkness of this world, and against spiritual wickedness in high places." You need the whole armour of God to fight against these enemies listed above. Physically, armour is a defensive covering used in battle. Without a complete armour, going into battle against the enemy is suicide. In 1Samuel 17, David used the most powerful armour, the name of the Lord of Host to defeat Goliath after rejecting the armour of King Saul.

What is your own armour? Charms, spiritual ring, satanic garment or have you been fortified by spiritual bath? All these will fail, "the name of the Lord is a strong tower, the righteous runneth into it, and is safe-Proverb 18:10. The enemies listed in Ephesians 6:12, all bow at the mention of the name of Jesus, because the name of Jesus is above every other names and a powerful weapon in warfare. For the weapon of our warfare are not carnal but mighty through God to the pulling down of strong holds- II Corinthians 10:4. You must be fully prepare before going into the battle field, preparation time is not a wasted time, make sure you are spiritually fit before confronting the enemy by recharging so that you can be in charge.

PRAYER BOMB

1. Father, I thank you for giving me victory over all my enemies, in Jesus name.
2. My Father, my maker, let all my enemies die mysteriously within 7 days from now, in Jesus name.
3. Father, let anyone or anybody that I s after my life, go mad, confess and die mysteriously, in Jesus name.
4. My Father my maker, anyone that needs to die for my life to be better, let the ground open and swallow the person, in Jesus name.
5. God of Elijah, arise by fire and roast to ashes anyone attacking me secretly anywhere, in Jesus name.
6. Divine arrow of sudden death from heaven, locate anybody that want me dead, in Jesus name.
7. You hired killer or assassin organized to kill me or any member of my family, sleep the sleep of the dead, in Jesus name.
8. Every Goliath troubling my life, business, marriage and family, I behead you now, in Jesus name.
9. Any witch or wizard attacking me in the spiritual realm, your time is up, give up the ghost, in Jesus name.
10. Lord of Host, arise in your anger and fight for me, in Jesus name.

11. Father, let every conspiracy against me in the air, land or sea, scatter by fire, in Jesus name.
12. Father, I release an incurable disease upon every household enemy and unfriendly friend that is after my life, in Jesus name.
13. Father, because life and death are in the power of my tongue, I decree death, upon anyone embarking upon an evil journey on my behalf, in Jesus name.
14. The God that answereth by fire, answer anybody calling my name in any shrine or altar by fire, in Jesus name.
15. Father, let any Calabash, pot, mirror the enemy is using to invoke my name for death, scatter by fire, in Jesus name.
16. Father, every source my enemy is getting power from to attack me, I dissolve the source, in Jesus name.
17. My Father, my maker, equip me with your armor, to confront every enemy that will come across me, in Jesus name.
18. Father, let any man or woman that need to die for me to live, in the name of Jesus, die by fire.
19. Sword of spirit, massacre anybody behind my entire predicament, in Jesus name.
20. My Father, my maker, let the announcement of the obituary of my enemies be announced one after the other from today, in Jesus name.

DAY FIVE

REVERSING THE CURSE IN YOUR LIFE TO BLESSING

Text: Deuteronomy 11: 26-28, Deuteronomy 39:19

Thunder Quote: (No man on earth can curse who God has blessed).

The choice you make in life matters a lot. Curse and blessing are choices that determine a man's destination. Giving your life to Jesus is not by force but by choice, because Salvation is a choice. The choice you make in life will either make or mar you. If you decide to serve the devil is a bad choice. Curse is the opposite of blessing. In Exodus 32, after Moses returned from the mountain into the camp of the children of Israel, he saw the people dancing in front of the image they constructed, representing their god, Moses anger waxed hot, he burnt the image and grounded it to powder, in verse 26 of Exodus 32 says, "then Moses stood in the gate of the camp and said, who is on the Lord's side? Let him come unto me."

The side you belong to is very important. Initially, a curse was pronounce upon Levi by his father, Jacob for killing a prince that defiled his sister Dinah, after the accused prince reconciled with their family. In Genesis 49, Jacob called all his children to tell them what will happen to them in the future, when it got to the turn of Levi he cursed him and the curse affected his destiny and his generation.

The day the Levites made a U-turn back to God, the curse upon them was reversed to blessing. When a man curses you, God can break the curse, but when God curse you, it is only God himself that can break the curse. No man on earth can curse who God has blessed. Zech 8: 13 says, "And it shall come to pass, that as ye were curse among the heathen house of Judah, house of Israel, so will I save you, and ye shall be a blessing." In respect of our text in Deuteronomy 30: 19, God says, "I call heaven and earth to record this day against you, that I have set before your life and death, blessing and cursing therefore choose life that both thou and thy seed may live" And in Deuteronomy 11: 27, God says "blessing if you will obey His commandment and a curse if you will not obey his commandment."

In nutshell, if you obey God, you are blessed and if you disobey God you are cursed. It is only God that has the power to change a curse into a blessing. In Nehemiah 13: 2b, scripture says, "Howbeit our God a turned curse into blessing". In Galatians 3: 13b, the Bible says, "Christ hath redeemed us from the curse of the law, being made a curse for us". Jesus Christ became a curse for you to be a blessing. If you want total deliverance from any curse, you must surrender totally to God. I have a good news for you, as you make up your mind to follow Jesus, every curse following you all these years, will be broken in Jesus name! And you won't see them again! By the power in the name of Jesus, today mark an end of every curse you have inherited, in Jesus name. I also decree by the auction placed on me and by the backing of the Trinity, I reverse every curse in your life, business, marriage, academic, family, finance to blessing, in Jesus name! Proverb 10: 22 says, "The blessing of the Lord, it maketh rich and he added no sorrow with it". I decree again, in that name that is above every other name, every curse that has brought poverty into your life is broken now, in Jesus name! Sorrow that accompanies curses will be far from you, in Jesus name! The day you realize who you are in Christ, you will know that curse is not your portion, because you are mandated to be a blessing as a seed of Abraham.

See what the Bible says about you in the book of Gen. 12: 2-3, "And I will make of thee a great nation, and I will bless thee, and make thy name great; and thou shalt be a blessing: And I will bless them that bless thee, and curse him that curseth thee." As a matter of fact, some people are blessed specially by God, no matter how you curse them, the curse won't work. In Number 22, King Balak was jealous because of the increase in the number of the children of Israel and he wanted to use his kingship authority on prophet Balaam so that he can pronounce curses upon the Israelite, but God spoke through the Prophet, How shall I curse, whom God hath not cursed? And the Bible says, in Number 23: 23b "Surely there is no enchantment against Israel Jacob, neither is there any divination against Israel."

From today I decree, you are a blessing to your family, Church, Nation, and the World, NOBODY can curse you, in Jesus name. Please ignore anything that can bring a curse upon you, especially SIN.

PRAYER BOMB

(1) Father, I thank you for reversing every curse in my life and family to blessing, in Jesus name.

(2) Father, every sin my forefather have committed that have brought curses upon me, O Lord, have mercy on me, in Jesus name.

(3) Father, anything that I've done in the past that is affecting me now, please have mercy on me, in Jesus name.

(4) Father, by the power in the name of Jesus, I reverse every curse in my life to blessing, in Jesus name.

(5) Father, every curse transferred into my life, through my father or mother, I break the curse, in Jesus name.

(6) Father, let every enchantment or divination against my destiny, receive the fire of the Holy Ghost, in Jesus name.

(7) Father, any ancient curse running in my family, I break the curse today, in Jesus name.

(8) Anyone or anybody that has placed a curse upon my destiny, your time has come, give up the ghost, in Jesus name.

(9) I release the fire and thunder of the Holy Ghost, into any shrine or altar anybody has used to place a curse upon me, in Jesus name.

(10) Father, I receive the divine blessing that maketh rich, in Jesus name.

(11) Father, let every man-made curse affecting the progress of my life break, in Jesus name.

(12) Father, every curse introduced into my life form birth, I destroy the curse now, in Jesus name.

(13) God of Elijah, release fire upon every stronghold of my enemy, wherever they are operating from, in Jesus name.

(14) Father, let every satanic power siphoning my finances; receive fire and scatter, in Jesus name.

(15) The anointing that breaks the yoke of curses, fall upon in my life, in Jesus name.

(16) Father, let every village curse affecting my progress in the city, break by fire, in Jesus name.

(17) Father, let any man or woman in any craft using my problem to gain promotion, die, in Jesus name.

(18) My Father, my maker, I release an incurable disease upon any man or woman calling my name for evil, in Jesus name.

(19) Holy Ghost fire, arise and consume every satanic handwriting upon my life, in Jesus name.

(20) My Father in heaven, turn every curse in my life, business, marriage, career, and family to blessing, in Jesus name.

DAY SIX

WAR AGAINST UNFRIENDLY FRIENDS AND HOUSEHOLD ENEMIES

Text: Psalm 41:5-9, Matthew 10:36

Thunder Quote :(Your friends determine your destiny.)

An adage says, "the ant that eats the leaf, lives inside the leaf." If you don't declare war against these two deadly enemies, they may end up killing you. Unfriendly friends and household enemies are enemies that live within a man. If you don't wage war against them on time, you may die an untimely death. In Ecclesiastes 3:8, the Bible says, "A time to love, and a time to hate, a time of war, and a time of peace." I guess, it is time to wage war against these deadly enemies, because their major mission is to make sure you die. If God doesn't deliver you from them, you are a dead man. Psalm 18:17 says, "He delivers me from my strong enemy, and from them which hate me for they were too strong for me." Another adage says, "if the enemy inside cannot kill you, the ones outside will not be able to kill you." The enemies outside get information from those inside before they attack. Before Jesus was arrested, an enemy within called Judas Iscariot gave the enemy information about him. That enemy within, that is giving information about you to your enemy to attack you, will die before sunrise tomorrow, in Jesus name!

These enemies are very close, they know almost everything about you; they know when and where you were born, they have details about you: where you live or where you work, they are informants to the enemy. In the book of Judges 16:16-21, when Samson foolishly revealed the secret of his power to Delilah, it became very easy for his enemies to capture him. The brothers of Joseph in Genesis 37, where the household enemy in his life, they hated him because of his great dream. Genesis 37:5 says, "And Joseph dreamed a dream, and he told it his brethren, and they hated him yet the more." There are some people you must not tell your dreams or vision, or else, you will end up in the grave with your dreams. A lot of people end up dead in the grave with great dream and vision because they foolishly use their own mouth to reveal their secret to the enemy. A particular woman believed God for the fruit of the womb for over 8 years, the day she carelessly told her friend that she is two months pregnant, before sunrise the following day she had a miscarriage.

Also, a young lady that was preparing for her wedding made a silly mistake by informing her step mother a day to her wedding, that wedding didn't hold because she didn't wake up to see her wedding day. I decree in the name of Jesus, any man or woman that has vowed that over their dead body will they see you get married, have children, graduated, be promoted or traveled abroad, may their obituary be announced within 24 hours from now, in Jesus name! A young guy that just came back to Nigeria from the UK visited his home town, he went round the town, greeting his families and also giving out money as well, unknown to him, one of his uncle that he gave money to took the money to a particular shrine, that was the end, he became a village boy. Listen, if you don't pray these enemies out of your life, they will stay in your life. I have stopped praying that my enemy should live and see what I will become in the future. I only pray that my enemy die and I will become what I want to be in the future. I discovered that the more you are progressing, the more your enemy will be reinforcing to truncate your destiny. The Bible says, in Exodus 22:18 "Thou shalt not suffer a witch to live." The fact that your enemy is still alive, you must be careful. In 1Samuel 16:1-14, David was made the new King, because King Saul disobeyed God, a form that day David didn't sit in the palace because Saul was after his life. After the death of King Saul in 11Samuel 2:4, David was re-anointed as King and he occupied his original position as the new King. I pray for you, anyone that needs to die for you to occupy your original position, may the ground open and swallow them, in Jesus name! Act 2:35 says, "Until I make thy foes thy footstool".

In 11King 7, Elisha prophesy a miraculous change into the land of Samaria due to the economy recession in the land, a particular man stood as a stumbling block, to his Prophesy, and he becomes a stepping stone. God will turn your enemy into a stepping stone to catapult you into your land of a miracle, in Jesus name.

There are some close friends that are our closest enemies in life, they eat with us, play with us, relate to us, and are the ones behind our problem. Psalm 41:8-9 says, "An evil disease, say they, cleaveth fast unto him: and now that he lieth he shall rise up no more. Yea, mine own familiar friends, in whom I trusted, which did eat of my bread, hath lifted up his heel against me." Some friends are betrayal, select your friends, it is not everyone that must be your friend because your friends determine your destiny. A friend of a thief is a thief. May the Almighty God separate you from every unfriendly friend and household enemy, in Jesus name! When you please God, he will make your enemies be at peace with you- Proverb 16:7. Receive divine grace from above to be above all, your enemies, in Jesus name.

PRAYER BOMB

(1) Father, I thank you for waging war against every unfriendly friend and household enemy who is after my life, in Jesus name

(2) Father Lord, let every unfriendly friend or household enemy, who is a witch or a wizard around me, confess and die, in Jesus name.

(3) Father, let every deadly enemy assigned from the pit of hell to destroy me, receive divining judgment and perish, in Jesus name.

(4) Father, let every unfriendly friend giving information about me to the enemy, be expose by fire and die, in Jesus name.

(5) Father, let anyone or anybody that is responsible for the present problem in my life, sleep and never wake up to see another day, in Jesus name.

(6) Father, give me the spirit of self-control so that I will not use my own mouth, to reveal my secret to the enemy, in Jesus name.

(7) Any man or woman that has vowed to make my life miserable, what are you living for, fall down and die, in Jesus name.

(8) Father, expose and bring to open shame anybody that is using charm or diabolical power to attack me secretly, in Jesus name.

(9) Father, let every unfriendly friend pretending to be my friend and he or she is attacking me secretly, receive the judgment of fire from heaven, in Jesus name.

(10) Father, let every agent of darkness in form of a friend in my life, receive fire and leave my life alone, in Jesus name.

(11) Father, use my enemies as a stepping stone to catapult me to the top, in Jesus name.

(12) Every household enemy holding me captive unknowingly to me, somersault and die wherever you are, in Jesus name.

(13) Father, give me the spirit of discernment to be able to discern between real friends, and unfriendly friends, in Jesus name.

(14) Father, expose by fire every secret hide out of my enemies, in Jesus name.

(15) My Father my maker, disappoint every secret agenda, the enemies are planning against my life, in Jesus name.

(16) Holy Ghost fire, locate and destroy anyone embarking on an evil journey to destroy my destiny, in Jesus name.

(17) Father, let anyone that has seen my glorious future, and want to abort it, somersault and die, in Jesus name.

(18) Father, deliver me from every destiny killer, that doesn't want me to reach my goal, in Jesus name.

(19) Father, let every satanic gadget the enemies are using to remote control my life, catch fire and scatter, in Jesus name.

(20) God of Elijah, incubate me with your fire against everyone that doesn't want me to fulfill my destiny, in Jesus name.

DAY SEVEN

BREAKING THE SATANIC YOKE UPON YOUR LIFE

Text: Mark 5:1-13

Thunder Quote: (A man carrying satanic load can never move faster in life.)

Agriculturally, a yoke is a frame in form of wood, placed upon animals for working together. Spiritually, yoke means something that restricts freedom. It can be satanic loads or evil property forced on someone to carry. A man carrying satanic load can never move faster in life, the load will restrict his movement. The yoke also means something that restricts freedom. A lot of people are moving like snail or tortoise on the earth because the yoke of slow motion is cast upon their destiny. They are always behind in life instead of being ahead; Journey of one hour will take them a day. The Satanic yoke can delay a man's destiny.

A particular young lady that just got married had a dream on the night of her honeymoon, after her wedding. She saw someone strange feeding her with cake the same way the groom feeds the bride during the wedding. After some months of waiting to conceive, she decided to go for a medical checkup and she was diagnosed of the fibroid, she went to operate the fibroid. After some months, She and her husband started believing God for the fruit of the womb again, and she decided to go for another medical checkup, and she was diagnosed that she had an appendix, she went for operation the second time and it was successful.

They decided to go for prayer in a particular Church, and a word came from the man of God that, there is a woman here that was fed with satanic meal in her dream after her wedding day to block her from conceiving, God has taken charge, today they are blessed with children after many years of waiting. Yokes are spiritual load, they are not physical, and it can only be handled spiritually. Many people are in the grave today because they applied the wrong formula to their problem. Imagine a problem that defies medical solution instead of going for prayer or deliverance you see people wasting resources, going from one hospital to the other, traveling abroad, at the end, some of them end up dead.

There are so many kinds of the yoke, the enemy can force upon someone, for example; curse, shame, poverty, reproach, bondage, failure, stagnation, barrenness, sickness, and disease. The same way human being put loads on camels back physically, that is the way the enemy forced load upon a human being in the spiritual realm. I pray for the readers of this book; every satanic load you have been carrying all these years, are destroyed now, in Jesus name! I also command, every owner of an evil load of your business, marriage or family to carry their load now, in Jesus name. May the yoke breaker "JESUS" break every yoke present in your life, in Jesus name!

Matthew 11:28-29, says, "Come unto me, all ye that labor and are heavy laden and I will give you rest, take my yoke upon you, and learn of me; for I am meek and lowly in heart, and ye shall find rest unto your souls." Working like an elephant and reaping like an ant is so common in the labor market today. I encountered a young man that told me that before he collects his salary at the end of every month, series of debt is waiting for him, and only about 20%

of his salary ends up in his hand, he is a man with children. When the yoke of hard labor is upon a man, he will be working hard without visible result. According to one of our definition of the yoke, something that restricts freedom. A lot of people are living a life in bondage. Some have been tied, caged and locked by the enemy not to move forward in life due to a satanic yoke of bondage. In John 5:1-9, a particular man suffered the yoke of bondage for 38 years, he was stagnated in one spot, he couldn't move until the yoke breaker stepped into his case, and he was liberated. I decree upon your life, that long standing issue in your life, will end today, and you will experience total freedom, in Jesus name.

Jesus is the only way out of that problem because he is the way according to John 14:6, and in John 8:36, the Bible says, "If the son, therefore, shall make you free, ye shall be free indeed." Receive total freedom from every Satanic bondage now, in Jesus name. That incurable sickness that has kept you in the bondage of sickness all these years is lifted now, in Jesus mighty name. With effect from today, your entire life is sickness free; you are loose and set free from every infirmity, in Jesus name. The yoke of infirmity disfigured a woman in Luke 13:10-13, for 18 years, she couldn't stand straight, she was in a C- shape position, the moment she encountered the God of all flesh, her body shape came back to the normal shape. Any problem in your life that has disfigured your life, marriage or business, I put an end to it now, in Jesus name! Your life will have a meaning again. The yoke of failure and lack of achievement is now the order of the day, many graduates are roaming about the street of our nation without jobs, some left the rural area to the city to hustle and are frustrated, the majority are busy business-men, without evidence to show forth. There is an anointing that comes from above that can break every yoke. In Isaiah 10:27, the Bible says, "And it shall come to pass in that day, that burden shall be taken away off thy shoulder, and his yoke from off thy neck, and the yoke shall be destroyed because of the anointing." By the power in the name of Jesus, I command every yoke in your life to be broken now, in Jesus name.

PRAYER BOMB

(1) Father Lord, I thank you for breaking every Satanic yoke upon my life, in Jesus name.

(2) Father Lord, let every satanic load the enemy has forced me to carry, catch fire, in Jesus name.

(3) Every yoke of the devil restricting my progress, scatter by fire, in Jesus name.

(4) Every spirit of snail or tortoise cast upon my life, come out now by fire, in Jesus name.

(5) God of Elijah, visit the source of my predicament by fire, in Jesus name.

(6) Father Lord, let every owner of the evil load in my life, carry their load now, in Jesus name.

(7) Father, any satanic yoke of sickness planted in my body, I uproot it by fire, in Jesus name.

(8) Father, let every arrow of untimely death shut against me, backfire to the sender, and kill the sender, in Jesus name.

(9) Anyone manipulating my destiny through dreams, your time is up surrendered and die, in Jesus name.

(10) My Father my maker, let anyone digging my grave when I am still alive, replace me and die, in Jesus name.

(11) Holy Ghost fire, enter my life and burn every satanic tree growing in my life, in Jesus name.

(12) The anointing that breaks the yoke, fall upon me now and break every generational yoke upon my destiny, in Jesus name.

(13) Father, every house of bondage the enemy has placed me; I escaped, in Jesus name.

(14) Any problem in the form on infirmity that has disfigured me from a normal human being, disappear by fire, in Jesus name.

(15) Anyone or anybody making life difficult for me, enough is enough; die by fire, in Jesus name.

(16) My Father my maker, break every yoke of hard labor, making me labor without visible result, in Jesus name.

(17) Father Lord, wherever the enemy has tied me, caged me or bind me, set me free, in Jesus name.

(18) Any problem that has stayed long in my life, receive expiring date, and expire, in Jesus name.

(19) Every power in the air, land or sea opposing my breakthrough, scatter by fire, in Jesus name.

(20) Jesus Christ of Nazareth, you are the yoke breaker, break every yoke upon my life now, in Jesus name.

DAY EIGHT

FORTIFY YOURSELF AGAINST BLOOD SUCKER

Text: Mark 5:24-29

Thunder Quote: (When you eat Jesus, you become uneatable to the enemy.)

One of the best drinks of witches and wizards is blood, they value blood more than wine because when they drink blood, the more they live longer. Principalities and powers understand Leviticus 17:11, that the life of the flesh is in the blood; so when they drink the blood of any human, they have taken life. The woman in our text in Mark 5:24-29, was losing life gradually because she was losing blood. She experienced abnormal menstruation for twelve years, equivalent to 4380 days. She has suffered in hand of many doctors, spent all she has, and the blood flow refuse to stop until she had an encounter with Jesus, the only one, who can put a final stop to any long standing problem.

Fortify means, to strengthen against attack, empowering yourself, to make yourself, to make yourself feel stronger or braver. You cannot win the enemy if you are not empowered by God. Ephesians 6:12 says, "For we wrestle not against flesh and blood, but against principalities, against powers, against the rulers of the darkness of this world, against spiritual wickedness in high places." If you don't want these enemies to eat your flesh or drink your blood, make sure you fortify yourself. There is no insurance in African insurance, (Charms or Juju) except in the name of Jesus. The Bible says, the name of Jesus is a strong tower, In 1 John 4:4, the Scripture says, "Ye are of God, little children, and have overcome them: because greater is he that is in you than he that is in the world." No Jesus, no life. John 6:53 says, "except ye eat the flesh of the Son of man and drink his blood, ye have no life in you." One of the best ways to fortify yourself is by constant partaking in the communion.

When you eat Jesus, you become uneatable to the enemy. There are some prayerless and powerless Christians that have ended up as food to the enemies because they refuse to recharge. They become prey to the enemy and end up in the belly of the enemy. Be a wise Christian, don't be ignorant of the devices of the devil, always have this in your mind, the devil's mission is to steal, to kill and to destroy, and you must be sober, and be vigilant always. Psalm 14:4 says "Have the workers of iniquity no knowledge? Who eat up my people as they eat bread and call not upon the Lord." How can a ritualist use you for ritual when you have fortified yourself.

The Bible says, touch not my anointed and do my Prophet no harm. A particular brother was kidnapped by ritualist, when they got to their altar of slaughter, they started killing people, when it got to the turn of this brother to be killed, they saw a wrist band on his right hand, and asked him, who are you? He answered, the son of Pastor Adeboye, they responded, bad market, that was how he escaped death. When you drink the blood of Jesus, it will dilute with your own blood, and your blood will become a supernatural blood, that becomes poison in the mouth of the enemy, like an acid. From today, your blood will become undrinkable to every blood sucker and every part of your body will become uneatable to flesh eaters, in Jesus name. Hear what God says about you in Isaiah 49:26a "And I will feed them that oppress thee with their own flesh and they shall be drunken with their own blood as sweet wine." I decree sudden death upon every blood sucker and flesh eaters after your life, in Jesus mighty name. Nobody will use you for sacrifice or money ritual, you will never be a victim of circumstances, in Jesus name. Because Jesus lives, you will live, you will not die, people will not gather to mourn you this year and I closed every door of condolence visit opened against you now, in Jesus name.

The communion is a special meal that fortifies against the enemy. When you take the communion, you become a fortified vessel, untouchable, unkillable, uneatable and a terror to the enemy. In the underworld, these deadly enemies are classified into two, Zombies and Vampires. Zombies are flesh eaters while vampires are the blood sucker.

When you are fortified, you become a dangerous Christian and a no go area to the enemy. In Galatians 6:17, the Bible says "From henceforth let no man trouble me, for I bear in my body the marks of the Lord." By the mandate of the Trinity, all the enemies you saw before embarking on this Spiritual exercise, you will not see them again, in Jesus name.

7 POWERFUL FORTIFIERS

1. The name of Jesus.
2. The blood of Jesus.

3. The Communion.
4. The word of God.
5. Fasting.
6. Prayer.
7. Praise.

PRAYER BOMB

1. Father, I thank you, for fortifying me against blood suckers and flesh eaters, in Jesus name.
2. Father, surround me with your wall of fire so that enemies will not come near me, in Jesus name.
3. Father Lord, let every flesh eater and blood sucker after my life, die mysteriously by fire, in Jesus name.
4. My Father my Father, let every long standing problem that has stayed long in my life, come to an end, in Jesus name.
5. Father, let every problem killing me gradually, receive fire and die now, in the name of Jesus.
6. Father, let every sickness or disease in my body defiling solution; dry up by fire, in the name of Jesus.
7. Father, every arrow of infirmity fired to end my life, lose target and locate your sender, in Jesus name.
8. Father Lord, my head, reject tragedy, calamity, disaster, evil news, in the name of Jesus.
9. Father, let every satanic mission of the enemy to truncate my vision; scatter by fire, in Jesus name.

10. Father, let every conclusion in the meeting of witches and wizards to attack me and my family, come to naught, in Jesus name.
11. Father, let every conspiracy against me from my village, place of work and neighborhood, be exposed, in Jesus name.
12. My maker my Father; I will not be a victim of circumstance or an object of caricature, in Jesus name.
13. Father, every gate of evil news and condolence visit opened against me, I close it permanently, in Jesus name.
14. Father, every trap of untimely death the enemy has prepared for me, I dismantle it, in the name of Jesus.
15. Father, I fortify myself with the blood of Jesus against every food poison prepared by any satanic cook, in Jesus name.
16. Father, let anyone or everyone that want me dead by all means, enter the ground and die, in Jesus name.
17. Father, I dissolve in the name of Jesus, every charms or Juju (black magic power) programmed to take my life, in Jesus name.
18. Father, put a final stop to every problem that wants to stop me from actualizing my destiny, in Jesus name.
19. Father, any journey of no return, don't let me embark upon it, in Jesus name.
20. Father, I decree and declare because Jesus Christ lives, I shall live, and I shall not die before my time, in the land of the living, in Jesus name.

DAY NINE

DIVINE REINFORCEMENT AGAINST SATANIC AGENTS

Text: Revelation 12:7-9

Thunder Quote: (You need help from above to be above of your enemy.)

No matter how powerful or spiritually equipped you may be, or think you are, you can't fight the enemy on your own, without divine help. No man is an island; it is only team work that makes the dream work. The Bible says, "woe to him that is alone." When you team up with God, forget it, you have won. Reinforcement from the dictionary means, sending extra soldiers to a place because more is needed. For instance when a particular number of soldiers are sent to rescue a particular state from the hand of a terrorist group, if they find it difficult to defeat the terrorist group, the soldiers must reinforce, if they don't want to end up all dead.

The moment you discover that the battle you're fighting is greater than you, please reinforced, so that you don't end up dead in the battle. As long as we are in this world, we can't run away from battles, because any battle you run from now awaits you in future. It is only a coward that retreat when he sees war. Life is no retreat, no surrender; you don't rest or go on holiday when you are on the battle field. In respect of our text in Revelation 12:7-9, the verse seven of it says, "And there was war in heaven. Michael and angels fought against the dragon: and the dragon fought back with his angels." I have often said that the kingdom of God suffereth violent, and only the violent taketh it by force. If you are gentle on the battle field, I pity you; your case will be like a fat cow in the midst of hungry lions. You must be ready to attack the enemy by positioning yourself, on the offensive side, if you desire victory in life. Please note, the day you become a born again Christian, that is, you renounced Satan, from that day, you become a target of the devil, he would do everything possible to bring you back into his fold to become his slave. In Exodus 14, immediately Pharaoh discovered that the children Israel had left Egypt, he became paranoid and said in verse 5 "why have we done this, that we have let Israel go from serving us." Pharaoh and his men regretted that they have made a big mistake to allowed the children of Israel go, they have to pursue them quickly. It grief's Satan when his victim escape.

I don't care how long you have been in the detention of the devil; you are free now, in Jesus name! That prison of affliction the enemy has kept you; I release you now, in Jesus name! Receive freedom, and be free indeed, in Jesus name. Because you have surrendered to the only one that can set someone free, receive total freedom, in every area of your life, in Jesus name. In 11Chronicles 20:1-25, three groups conspired against Jehoshaphat to battle, he had to reinforced by inviting the mighty man in battle into scene by singing praises to the Almighty God, their praises moved God, He laid ambush against the three groups that conspired against Jehoshaphat, they started killing themselves, and when Judah came to the battle field, there were dead bodies of all the three groups scattered everywhere, it took Jehoshaphat and his men three days to carry all their spoils of precious Jewels that they stripped off from the dead bodies of the three groups. In Isaiah 19:2, the Bible says, "And I will set the Egyptians against the Egyptians: and they shall fight every one against his brother, and every one against his neighbor: city against city and kingdom against kingdom." Every conspiracy against you in the air, land or sea, shall scatter for your sake, in Jesus name! God will arise for you today, and scatter every Satanic gathering against your business, marriage, and family, in Jesus name. You need help from above to be above your enemy, because of our number one enemy the devil is desperate, looking for means to fulfill his three fold ministry, to kill, steal and destroy. May you never be a victim of the devil, in Jesus name!

Many Christians are not wise, that is the reason why they end up as food in the belly of the enemy. The Bible says we should be wise as a serpent. To survive in this wicked world, your spiritual antenna must be at work always and must be spiritually sensitive because our enemy the devil is very wise and tricky. When the devil discover that you have known his trick, he will change his strategy. Receive divine wisdom to discern every trick of your enemy, in Jesus name. In the battle field, it is either you win or the enemy wins, there is nothing like drawing, someone must be the winner, you win, and live or lose and die, the choice is yours. I pray that you will always win in any match between you and the enemy, in Jesus name.

Because you are on the Lord's side, you are on the winning side; God will fight for you, in Jesus name. There are some battles you can't fight and win on your own without God on your side. By strength shall no man prevail, it's not by power nor by might; you need God to win in any battle. The world is likened to a battle ring, your opponent is the devil and the only way you can win is, by inviting God to take over the battle, when God takes over, it is over. It is written in Exodus 14:14, "The Lord shall fight for you, and ye shall hold your peace." If God is on your side, who can be against you? God will take over, every battle in your life and it will be over, in Jesus name. In Joshua 10:5-26, five kings teamed up together against Gibeon, and the men of Gibeon sent for Joshua to come and assist them in the battle, Joshua had to reinforce by inviting God into the battle and God took over and at the end, five kings died by hanging. May God arise on your behalf as you invite him into that battle, in Jesus name!

PRAYER BOMB

1. Father, I thank you for sending reinforcement from above to me, in Jesus name.
2. Father, please send angelic reinforcement from above to me to rescue me, from every battle of life, in Jesus name.
3. Father, I cannot fight the enemy by myself, please arise and fight for me, in Jesus name.
4. My ministering angels encamped round about me now, and begin to fight for me, in Jesus name.
5. Father, arise and fight all the enemies that have teamed up to attack me, in Jesus name.
6. My Father my Father, I hand over every battle of my life to you, please take over and let all be over, in Jesus name.
7. The God that rescue Paul and Silas in the prison, please rescue me from the prison of the enemy, in Jesus name.
8. God of Elijah, arise by fire and set me free, from every satanic bondage the enemy has kept me all these years, in Jesus name.
9. My enemies, in the name of Jesus, begin to kill yourselves by yourselves, in Jesus name.

10. Father, I need help from above, that will make me be above all my enemies, in Jesus name.
11. Father, let every conspiracy against me from the coven of witches and wizard, scatter by fire, in Jesus name.
12. Father, grant me the spirit of discernment against every trick of the enemy, in Jesus name.
13. My Father my Father, prove to my enemy that you are on my side, by giving me victory, in Jesus name.
14. Holy thunder, fire and earthquake descend upon all my enemies wherever they are, in Jesus name.
15. God that answereth by fire, let your fire fall and consume every long existing problem in my life, in Jesus name.
16. Father, let every plan of the devil to take my life, in the battle field fail, in the name of Jesus.
17. Father, let every spirit of death roaming about in my family receive the fire of God and leave now, in Jesus name.
18. Father Lord, give me the power to dominate in the physical and spiritual realm, in Jesus name.
19. Father, let every satanic informant assigned to monitor my life, business, and marriage, die by fire, in Jesus name.
20. Father, let every house of bondage, caging my glory, business, and marriage, receive fire and release me, in Jesus name.

DAY TEN

WAKE UP FROM YOUR SLUMBER

Text: Proverbs 6:6-11

Thunder Quote: (The future awaiting a lazy man is regret.)

A lot of people sleep too much, no wonder their miracle slip out from their hands. Too much sleeping will land a man in the valley of poverty. It is better to work now and play later than to play now and work later. If you refuse to work hard now, the future will be hard, if you fail to plan, your future plan will fail. Proverbs 21:25 says,"the desire of the slothful killeth him, for his hand refuse to labor."

Listen, hard work is a part of life. Proverb 19:15 says, "Slothfulness casteth into a deep sleep and an idle soul suffer hunger." No food for a lazy man, God cannot bless a lazy man, but the devil can use him if he is idle, because an idle man is the devil's workmanship. Proverb 19:24 says, "A slothful man hideth his hand in his bosom, and will not so much as bring it to his mouth again." What you do now will determine your future, if you can pay the price now; a prize of greatness awaits you in the future.

No cross, no glory, no pain, no gain. Napoleon Hill says many people wish for riches, but few provide a definite plan and the burning desire that lead to wealth. The only future awaiting a lazy man is regret, if you are not willing to pay sacrifice, greatness may end in your lips. A lazy man lives so slowly that poverty catches up with him. Those who do nothing today end up being nothing tomorrow.

What is an ant? According to Proverbs 30:24-25, "There be four things which are little upon the earth, but they are exceeding wise: The ants are a people not strong, yet they prepare their meat in the summer." Also, Oxford Dictionary defined Ant as a small insect that lives in a highly organized group. Take an ant called termite for example, that have a king, a queen, workers, and soldiers, they are organized, when it is time to work, the workers and soldiers team up together and work without supervision. If an ordinary Ant can work, you must wake up and work.

George Burns says; "don't stay on the bed unless you can make money on the bed." If you can't make money on the bed, get up and go to the place you can make money. A lazy man will still complain even when success is at his door, and a lazy man will always quarrel with his tools. Many old people are leaving in regret because they fail to pay the price in their youth days. "It is good for a man that he bears the yoke in his youth-Lamentations 3:27. Don't use the time of planning to play, there is time for everything when your mate is working, make sure you work if you don't want to be a liability in the future.

In Ecclesiastes 2:17b, the Bible says "there is a time for every work." There is a time to work and a time to retire, don't use your retire time as a working time. Today, we see many old people in the labor market hustling with the youth instead of being in their villages resting, what they are supposed to do, they failed to do it. Anything you find difficult to do now, will be hard to do in the future, imagine a man of 70 years old going back to school, what you have to do, do quick, tick says the clock. If you want to eat big food, you must be ready to work. Pastor Sam Adeyemi says it only fools that eat all their harvest, learn how to invest some of your harvest for future purpose. If you are lazy, success will run from you, even money doesn't stay in the hand of lazy people. Life cannot accommodate lazy people. Romans 12:11 says "Not slothful in business, fervent in spirit, serving the LORD," Jesus says, my Father worketh hitherto I work, John 9:4. Many of us are suffering today due to the seed of laziness owned by our parents; a lazy father will produce a lazy son.

A lazy man will wake up very late, go out for his business very late, misses early customers that bring early fat money for the business transaction. Ben Franklin says, early to bed and early rise makes a man healthy, wealthy and wise. The enemy use opportunity to destroy destiny when people sleep. In Matthew 13:25, "But while men slept, his enemy came to sowed tares among the wheat, and went his way."

5 PEOPLE IN THE BIBLE THAT WERE DILIGENT

(1) David was a committed shepherd before he became a King-1 Sam 16:11-14.
(2) Elisha was a faithful farmer before he became a Prophet-1 King. 19:19-21.
(3) Peter was professional fisherman before he became one of the disciples-Matthew 4:18-2.
(4) Dorcas was a fashion designer-Act 9:36-40.

(5) Rachael was a shepherd taking care of her father's sheep-Gen 29:9.

Great men in our generation that invented most of the things we are benefiting from today paid the price of making research. Researchers don't sleep the way other people sleep; they are always awake at night putting brain at work in other to have resulted. I command, in that name that is above every other name, every spirit of slumber affecting your destiny to come out by fire, in Jesus name. Act 20:7-12, Paul was preaching and a man called Eutychus was sitting on the window, and he fell asleep and fell down from the upper chamber and died and Paul restored him back alive, may you not sleep the sleep of death, in Jesus name.

PRAYER BOMB

(1) Father, I thank you for waking me up from every spiritual slumber, in Jesus name.
(2) My inner man, receive fire and come alive, in Jesus name.
(3) My Father my creator, wake me up from every slumber, in Jesus name.
(4) Father, let every spirit compelling me to sleep so that I can be poor in life, leave my life by fire, in Jesus name.
(5) Father, I receive power from heaven to pay the price of greatness so that I can be great, in Jesus name.
(6) Father, please don't let me sleep the sleep of death, in Jesus name.
(7) My Father, my creator, let every time waster that wants to waste my time without achieving a result, leave my life, in Jesus name.

(8) Father, let every spirit of idleness in my life; come out by fire, in Jesus name.
(9) My destiny, arise and shine from glory to glory, in Jesus name.
(10) My Father my creator, every seed of laziness planted in my life, I uproot it by fire, in Jesus name.
(11) Father Lord, give me a wisdom that exceeds the wisdom of men, in Jesus name.
(12) Father, give me a fervent spirit so that I won't be slothful in life, in Jesus name.
(13) Father, breathe life upon everything that is dead in my life, in Jesus name.
(14) Father, please position me at the right place of the miracle at the right time, in Jesus name.
(15) Father, pull me out of every pit of complaining the enemy has put me, in Jesus name.
(16) Father, every darkness surrounding my glory, vanish by fire, in Jesus name.
(17) Father, give me an excellent spirit to excel in life, in Jesus name.
(18) My Father my father, let your light of glory shine upon my life, and remove every shame from my life, in Jesus name.
(19) Father, let every storm of poverty affecting my prosperity calm down by fire, in Jesus name.
(20) Father, I receive the power to be diligent in every ramification of life, in Jesus name.

DAY ELEVEN

FREEDOM FROM SATANIC PRISON

Text: Mark 5:1-13

Thunder Quote: (When you become violent, prisons will open.)

Satanic Prison is the worst prison to ever be because the owner of the prison is Lucifer and it is controlled by his agents. Freedom means, the state of being able to do what you want without anyone stopping you, or when someone is not a prisoner or a slave.

Prison is a building where people are kept as a punishment for a crime they have committed or while they are waiting for trial. It also means a place or situation from which somebody cannot escape. Spiritually, a prison is a place of affliction, torment, pains, suffering, captivity, sorrow and bondage. According to our Bible text, the mad man of Gadara was living in a tomb for many years, his own madness was extraordinary, because whenever he was chained, he would break the chain. He became violent that they have to abandon him. The devil tormented him every time, he would be crying and cutting himself with a stone until one fateful day when he met Jesus; the one that can set the captive free, that day he got his freedom. I don't know how long you have stayed in that satanic prison; receive freedom now, in Jesus name.

We have two major types of prison

(1) Physical Prison: This prison is prepared for law breakers like thieves, murderers, kidnappers, terrorists, etc.

(2) Spiritual Prison: it is a prison where destinies are tied, glories are captured, businesses, marriages, and dreams are detained by the devil and agents of darkness.
The Spiritual Prison is ruled and controlled by the spiritual world, the god of this world Lucifer, demon, witches and wizards, marine powers, in nutshell, the devil, and his agents. In the Spiritual Prison, the forces of darkness carry out their operations in the morning, afternoon and night to fulfill their satanic mission; to steal, to kill, and to destroy in John 10:10a. I pray for you reading this book, every satanic agenda plotted against you is destroying, in Jesus name!

SOME COMMON SPIRITUAL PRISONS ARE:

(1) Prison of affliction; the woman with the issue of blood, in Luke 8:43-48.
(2) Prison of failure; Jabez, in I Chronicles 4:9-10.
(3) Prison of poverty; the widow of Zaraphat, in 1kings 17:8-16.
(4) Prison of Sickness; the man that was sick for 38 years, in John 5:2-9.
(5) Prison of Death; Lazarus, in John 11:1-44.
(6) Prison of Fear; Israel and the Philistine, in 1Samuel 17:1-11.

(7) Prison of Debt; the widow whose husband was a Prophet, in 11kings 4:1-7.
(8) Prison of Bondage; the children of Israel spent 430 years, in Egypt.
(9) Prison of Generational Curse; Naomi's family, in Ruth 1:1-5.
(10) Prison of Bareness; Hannah, in 1Samuel 1:1-20.

God is aware of the prison you find yourself, have faith, he will make a way of escape for you in that prison because he did it for Peter in Act 12:5-11, by sending an angel to rescue him, also in Act 16:25-26, he delivered Paul and Silas. You are not the first person to be in that prison, study what ex-prisoners did to be liberated. Complain, weeping and crying cannot take you out but when you decide to be violent like Paul and Silas, you will come out of that prison. When you become violent, prisons will open.

WHAT DO I DO WHEN I FIND MYSELF IN THE PRISON

1. Examine yourself, check if you are guilty or innocent.
2. Don't stop praying, pray until you are out of the prison- 1Thessalonians 5:17.
3. Make sure you have people praying for you, prayer partners- Act 12:5b, 12b.
4. Focus on your assignment- Act 5:16-42.
5. Have faith in God.
6. Praise/Worship God continually.
7. Give thanks to God- I Thessalonians 5:18.

The only person that can set you free from that satanic prison is Jesus according to John 8:36, "If the son, therefore, shall make you free, ye shall be free indeed." Run to him now, like the mad man of Gadara in our text, worship him and you shall receive your freedom.

PRAYER BOMB

(1) Father, I thank you for setting me free, from every satanic prison, in Jesus name.
(2) Father, I escape now from every satanic detention, in Jesus name.
(3) In the name of Jesus, I am free from every satanic manipulation, in Jesus name.
(4) My Father my creator, let every garment of the prisoner that the enemy has forced on me, catch fire, in Jesus name.
(5) Father, send angelic help to deliver me from the hand of every principality and power, in Jesus name.
(6) Father, every cage caging my glory, star, and my destiny, scatter by fire, in Jesus name.
(7) Father, every Iron Gate locking me out of miracles, I uproot it by fire, in Jesus name.
(8) Father, let every door that leads to my breakthrough, open by fire, in Jesus name.
(9) Father, let every satanic guard or security assigned to monitor me, sleep and die, in Jesus name.
(10) My Father my creator, don't let me die, in the prison of untimely death, in Jesus name.
(11) Father, raise prayer partners for me, whenever I find myself in any satanic prison, in Jesus name.

(12) Father, let every satanic warehouse housing my blessing, receive fire and release my blessing to me, in Jesus name.

(13) Father, let every satanic wander afflicting my life; receive fire and die, in Jesus name.

(14) Father, let every prison of poverty the enemy has put me, receive earthquake from heaven and scatter now, in Jesus name.

(15) Father, I sentence every enemy that is after my life, to life imprisonment, in Jesus name.

(16) Holy Ghost thunder and earthquake strike to death, anyone making incantation against me, in any altar or shrine, in Jesus name.

(17) God of Elijah, arise by fire and consumed by fire, every household enemy, giving information about me, to the enemy in Jesus name.

(18) My Father my creator, let every power of darkness troubling my life, become powerless now, in Jesus name.

(19) Father, every file of the prisoner, I delete my name from it, in Jesus name.

(20) The God that delivered Paul and Silas from the prison of the enemy, arise and deliver me from every satanic prison, in Jesus name.

DAY TWELVE

RECHARGE AND BE IN CHARGE

Text: 1 Kings 19:1-8

Thunder quote: (The time you spend in recharging will determine your performance.)

There are some wicked and dangerous enemies you can't confront or challenge, if you have not fully recharge spiritually or else, you will end up dead. The moment you recharge, you will be fit for any battle. When you recharge spiritually, you will become a terror and a dangerous person to your enemy. A rechargeable lamp needs current to recharge so that it can give light when input in power supply fails and darkness appears. Don't ever go into the battle field if you have not recharged or else you will die in the battle field. In our Bible text, in the previous Chapter, Elijah killed four hundred and fifty Prophets of Baal that contested with him, and Ahab told Jezebel, she became angry, and was after Elijah according to her response in 1 Kings 19:2, "Then Jezebel sent a messenger unto Elijah, saying, so let the gods do to me, and more also, if I make not thy life as the life of one of them by tomorrow about this time."

Jezebel vowed that within 24 hours, Elijah will also die, she boasted with her god against Elijah, and Elijah ran for his life. Imagine a man that killed 450 Prophets of Baal and just a woman threatened him, and he was afraid. That strong man or strong woman intimidating your life will die today, in Jesus name. Receive the spirit of boldness to confront your enemies, in Jesus name! I pray for you, from today anyone boasting with the negative power to threaten your life will fall and die, in Jesus name. Elijah acted in a coward way because virtue had gone out of him, he just killed 450 people and he has not recharge to face their head, Jezebel. After the end of every battle, you need to recharge to remain in charge or else you will lose in the next match. A powerless man is an easy prey to the enemy. I decree into your life; power to win in every battle; receive it now, in Jesus name. Elijah became frustrated because he didn't realize that he had not recharged to face his enemy, he entertained the spirit of fear and he became afraid of Jezebel. The Bible says, fear hath torment according to 1John 4-18b. If you allow fear to your life, you will be tormented. I chase away every spirit of fear that has given the devil power to torment you out, in Jesus name. In the process of running away from his enemy, Elijah ran into the wilderness, he told God to take his life. I don't know the situation you are going through now, and you think suicide is the way out, may God step into that situation, in Jesus name!

Elijah slept off in the wilderness and God sent a rescue team to him, they gave him angelic meal twice and he was empowered, his spiritual battery became fully recharged and was able to spend forty days and forty nights on the mountain. If you are not endued with power from above, you will be defeated in the battle field. Isaiah 40:31 says, "But they wait upon the LORD shall renew their strength; they shall mount up with wings as eagles; they shall run, and not be weary, and they shall walk and not faint." If you watch the life of eagles, whenever they discovered that most of their feathers have removed from their bodies, they will fly to a very high mountain and stay there for a period of time until their feathers grow, and they will start flying again. After Peter denied

Jesus three times, he went to recharge and became bold, the spirit of fear departed from him, and in Act 2:38-41, he preached just a sermon and 3,000 souls were saved. The moment you recharge, an extraordinary power will come upon you to do extra ordinary. Daniel 11:32b says, "But the people that do know their God shall be strong, and do exploits." The time you spend in recharging will determine your performance. You can't compare someone who spends 7 days with God and someone who spends 7 minutes, the difference is clear. In Exodus 34:28-35, after Moses spent 40 Days and 40 Nights with God, he transformed into another person to the extent that nobody can look into his face until he had to put a veil upon his face. You need power from above to challenge principalities and powers.

The Kingdom of God is not in word but in a demonstration of power. If you lack power, you will lack authority. The day you receive Jesus into your life, you have received power, John 1:12. Receiving Jesus is the first step to recharge if you desire to be in charge. When your destiny is cemented on the power of God, you will be in charge of your enemies. There is a greater power in you as a bonafide child of God. 1John 4:4 says, "Because greater is he that is in you, than he that is the world." The power that you carry inward determines your outward manifestation.

10 WAYS TO RECHARGE AND BE IN CHARGE

(1) Connect to the source of all power-John 1:12.

(2) Build the word of God into your life- Colossian 3:16.

(3) Love righteousness and hate sin- Psalm 45:7.

(4) Fast regularly- Matthew 4:1-4.

(5) Pray violently- James 5:16.

(6) Partaking in the communion regularly-John 6:53.

(7) Go into high praise- Act 16:24-26.

(8) Thirst and hunger for power-Matthew 5:6.

(9) Constant fellowship with the Holy Spirit- Galatians 5:25.

(10) Spend quality time in God's presence- Isaiah 40:31.

PRAYER BOMB

1. Father, I thank you for recharging my spiritual life with your fire against every attack of the enemies, in Jesus name.
2. God of Elijah, overshadow me with your fire and make me untouchable against the kingdom of darkness, in Jesus name.
3. Father, let every extinguisher assigned from the pit of hell to put off my fire, receive fire and perish, in Jesus name.
4. Father, baptize me with fresh fire, from above to become a terror to all my enemies, in Jesus name.
5. My Father my creator, you answered Elijah by fire when he called unto you, answer me now by fire, in Jesus name.
6. Father, let every Jezebel, Pharaoh, Herod or Goliath after my life, fall down and die, in Jesus name.
7. Father, let every evil wall of partition between me and my breakthrough collapse by fire, in Jesus name.
8. Father, anyone or anybody boasting with evil powers to intimidate me, your time is up, die by fire, in Jesus name.

9. Father, I receive power from above to be above all my enemies, in Jesus name.
10. My ministering angels, feed me with angelic food that turns an ordinary person into an extraordinary person, in Jesus name.
11. Father, every journey programmed to take my life; I refuse to embark upon, in Jesus name.
12. My Father my creator, go ahead of me and make every great journey ahead of me, safe trip, in Jesus name.
13. Father, cover me with your glory that attracts favor before man and woman that matters, in life in Jesus name.
14. Father, let every satanic messenger or post master assigned to bring evil news to me, somersault and die, in Jesus name.
15. Father, let every spirit of cowardliness in my life; die by fire, in Jesus name.
16. God of Elijah, recharge my entire life with your fire to be in charge in every ramification of life, in Jesus name.
17. The anointing that breaks the yoke, fall upon me now and break every yoke in my life, in Jesus name.
18. Power to heal the sick, raise the dead, deliver the oppressed, set the captives free and to tread upon serpents and scorpions, fall upon me, in Jesus name.
19. Holy Ghost fire, activate my body, spirit, and soul with your fire, in Jesus name.
20. My Father my maker, connect me back to the socket of power to become a powerful Christian, in Jesus name.

DAY THIRTEEN

HOW OLD IS YOUR PROBLEM?

Text: John 5:2-9

Thunder Quote: (Problem can only delay you temporarily, but you can stop yourself permanently.)

From our text above, the man in our text had been sick for 38 years, that is to say, the sickness in his life is 38 years old. The Bible didn't tell us the man's age, however, he has been in the condition for a long time with his friends that are disabled. In respect of the protocol, an angel will come down in a particular season into the pool, stair the water and the first person to step into the water among the disabled people will be made the whole of whatsoever disease he had. I guess this man's problem is the oldest, and Jesus had to step into his case, Jesus by-passed the normal protocol and that was the end of the 38 years infirmity. I don't care how old that problem in your life may be, today marks the end, in Jesus name!

The fact that you are born again doesn't exclude you from challenges of life. Life is a learning field. Problems and crises are storms you will encounter in the journey of life. Storms never give notice before they strike, they can come anytime. It is not how long you have stayed in that problem but how well. Hear the story of this man called Debo, he said, ''before I gave my life to Christ in the year 2001, I was infected with STD, which I contacted due to carelessness with a prostitute. I carried the disease for years, on the night of my honeymoon in 2008 with my wife, I started rolling on the floor, asking God for mercy in respect of what I have done in the past, instead of going into business with my wife, suddenly, I felt relief in my body, that was the end of STD in my life, that sickness was almost ten years old."

Note, the fact that Jesus is in your boat doesn't mean you won't experience storms, you will, but you won't sink because, God promised us in Isaiah 43:2a that, when thou passest through the waters, I will be with thee; and through the rivers, they shall not overflow thee. Those marine powers, that want to sink the boat of your life, I command them to perish in the sea, in Jesus name. Every problem has manufacturing date and expiring date, by power in the name of Jesus; I command that problem in your life to expire now! I have no doubt, you will testify before sunset today.

No condition is permanent; every problem has a solution, receive a solution to that problem that you cannot share with your fellow human, in Jesus name. In 1Peter 5:10, God says, after you have suffered for a while, he will settle you. Receive divine settlement for all your suffering, in Jesus name. II Corinthians 4:17, says,"for our light afflictions, which is for a moment worketh for us far more exceeding and eternal weight of glory. Problems can only delay you temporarily but you can stop yourself permanently. Delay is not denial. Don't give up because of what you are going through now, there is still hope tomorrow. You will break through what you are passing through, in Jesus name. God never promised us an easy journey in life but only safe arrival. A road without a road blocker does not lead to any important destination. There is nobody living in this world without a problem. Any man on earth without a problem is a problem on earth. I see heaven releasing solution to that problem resisting solution in your life, in Jesus name! Receive help from above, in Jesus name.

SOME LONG STANDING PROBLEM GOD SOLVED

1. Act 9:32-34- Aeneas suffered stroke for 8 years on the bed, God used Peter to heal him, and that was the end of stroke in the life of Aeneas.

2. Mark 5:25-34- A particular woman with an issue of blood had an unstoppable flow of blood from her private part for 12 years, after an encounter with Jesus, the unstoppable blood stopped, and the end came to 12 years old infirmity.

3. Luke 13:10-14- A woman had the spirit of infirmity for 18 years, she could not raise her head up rightly because she had a problem with her spinal cord, Jesus touched her and she became straight.

4. Act 3:1-9, Act 4:2- A man born lame from birth, he could not walk, God used Peter to restore him, he is over 40 years old, that is to say, the problem is over 40 years old.

5. John 5:1-9- The man by the pool of Bethesda was sick for 38 years, Jesus stepped into his case and 38 years old problem vanished.

How many years have you suffered from barrenness, joblessness, failure, poverty, delay, sickness, demotion, shame, reproach and a generational curse, Jesus will step in and all will be over, in Jesus name.

PRAYER BOMB

1. Father, I thank you because every problem that has overstayed in my life is gone forever, in Jesus name.
2. Father, any known and unknown problem growing with me day by day, today mark your end, disappear now, in Jesus name.
3. My Father my maker, let every old problem that is older than me, die by fire, in Jesus name.
4. Father, arise by fire and terminate every satanic plant growing in my body, in Jesus name.
5. My Father, my Creator, by-pass every protocol and man-made law and set me totally free from the generational curse, in Jesus name.
6. Oh Lord my God, every problem in my life that is bringing mockery to your name, take it away by fire, in Jesus name.
7. Every association of nonentity, I found myself, I come out speedily, in Jesus name.
8. You spirit of poverty, failure, joblessness, sickness, and reproach, you have stayed long in my life, I command you to leave, in Jesus name.
9. Father, put an end to every endless problem in my life today, in Jesus name.
10. Father, don't let me end up dead in my problem, please intervene quickly and help me, in Jesus name.

11. Father, every atrocity that I have done in the past that is affecting your original plans in my life, please have mercy on me in Jesus name.
12. Father, let every satanic problem manufactured by my business, marriage, and family, expire now, in Jesus name.
13. Father, let every problem that has turned into a mountain in my life, scatter by fire, in Jesus name.
14. Father, any problem I can't share with my fellow human, I hand it over to you today, in Jesus name.
15. Father, let every power of delay, delaying me from fulfilling a destiny, become powerless, in Jesus name.
16. Father, release the solution to every problem in my life to me, in Jesus name.
17. Father, I have waited for enough, please answer me now by fire, in Jesus name.
18. Father, every queue of stagnation and delay the enemy has placed me; I jump out by fire, in Jesus name.
19. Father, position me on the fast lane in the journey of life, in Jesus name.
20. Father, let every road blocker from the pit of hell assigned to stop me from reaching my destination, die by fire, in Jesus name.

DAY FOURTEEN

SET THAT EVIL GARMENT ABLAZE

Text: Zechariah 3:1-4

Thunder Quote: (People will address you according to the way you dress.)

You are what you wear, and your dressing reflects your personality. People will address you according to the way you dress. If you dress like a gentle man, you will be addressed in a gentle way, but if you decide to dress like a thug, you will be addressed like a thug. Some people are wearing designer's clothes physically, but spiritually they are wearing rags. In reference to our Bible text, Joshua was an ordained high priest of the Lord, he was supposed to be wearing a priest garment, but the devil used a satanic garment to cover his real priestly garment.

There are satanic garments imported from the pit of hell into the earth, which is the reason why you must be careful the kind of clothes you buy and where you purchase the clothes. I always pity people that buy fairly used clothes at night, listen, the world is full of wickedness and a lot of people have been initiated or afflicted through clothes they bought. A young bachelor and his sister were living together in a room apartment, one day the guy went to the market to buy a fairly used boxer short in the market. Any night he wears the boxer short, his manhood will rise, and he will be sexually aroused to have sex with his sister. One day, he was in a praying program, and a word came from the man of God, that, he is being manipulated by the devil to commit an abomination with his own blood sister. Immediately he got home, he set the boxer short on fire and that was the end.

I don't know that Satanic garment that you bought or someone gave you that the enemy is using to manipulate your destiny, I set it ablaze now, in Jesus name. A particular lady just moved into an apartment, she washed her clothes and her under wear, spread them on a rope and went out for her business. When she came back from work, she couldn't find one of her pants that she washed, after three days, she found the pant, she was not sensitive spiritually, and she took the pant into her room. The day she wore the pant, her menstruation period seized. I have often said, we are in a very wicked world, the enemies are going the extra mile to truncate people's destiny. For instance, a woman got pregnant and someone gave her evil wrapper, unknowingly to her, the day she wore the wrapper, she started bleeding, and was rushed to the hospital, finally she had a miscarriage.

Has anyone taking anything that belongs to you, and they are using it to torment you, the God of Elijah will turn it to fire in their hands until they return it back to you the way it was, in Jesus name. Anything the enemy has forcefully collected from you, receive it back now, in Jesus name. Once again, be careful and beware, we are in a deadly world that is full of many enemies and few friends. Don't be a careless and sleeping Christian, be wise and open your eyes, be sober and be vigilant, watch and pray always. Matthew 10:16 says, "Behold, I send you forth as sheep in the midst of wolves, be ye, therefore, wise as a serpent and harmless as doves."

7 SATANIC GARMENTS PEOPLE WEARS

1. The garment of Bondage: In Genesis 37:3, the father of Joseph made a garment of many colors for him initially, but the enemy doesn't want him to fulfill his destiny, they tore his garment and sold him to slavery. He landed in the prison wearing prisoners garment. God remember him in Genesis 41:14 after he was released from prison, they changed the prison garment to VIP attire.

2. The garment of Widowhood: This very common in the world. Most couple's don't mark 30th or 40th Wedding Anniversary like in the olden days. Death knows that two is better than one, two will chase ten thousand, and that there is power in the agreement between two people. In Genesis 38; Tamar the daughter-in-law of Judah became a widow in her early days in verse 19, she put on a garment of a widow. Also in the book of Ruth Chapter one; Naomi's husband died and she became a widow. May you and your spouse live long and see your children's, in Jesus name.

3. The garment of Poverty: This garment is one of the most popular garments in the world. Jabez wore the garment in 1Chronicles 4:9-10, Gideon also wore the garment in Judges 6:15. Two widows also wore the garment of poverty in 1kings 17:10-12 and 11 Kings 4:1-7.

4. The garment of Failure: One of the individuals in the scripture that wore the garment of failure is Peter in Luke 5:1-7. He went

to work and came back without result. When the garment of failure is upon anyone, success will run from the person.

5. The garment of Barrenness: Sarah, Elizabeth, Rachael, and Hannah are an example of women that wore the garments of barrenness before God made them mothers of children. I pray for you reading this book by this time next year, you will embrace your own baby, in Jesus name.

6. The garment of Sickness or Disease: The woman with the issue of blood in Luke 8:43-48, wore the garment for 12 years. The man with infirmity beside the pool of Bethesda in John 5:1-9, wore his own for 38 years. I don't know how long you have been wearing that garment of sickness, today marks the end, I command that garment to catch fire, in Jesus name.

7. The garment of Generational Curse: In II Kings 5:21-27, because of greed Gehazi brought a generational curse upon his children. Lamentation 5:7 says, "Our fathers have sinned and we are not, and we have borne their iniquities."

POWER BOMB

(1) Father, I thank you for setting ablaze every satanic garment upon my life, in Jesus name.

(2) Father, every satanic garment the enemy has forced upon me; I pull it off and set it ablaze, in Jesus name.

(3) Father, let every principality and power resisting me from accessing my miracles, perish by fire, in Jesus name.

(4) My Father, my creator, change every filthy garment in my life into a royal garment, in Jesus name.

(5) Father, let any satanic thief assigned to steal anything in my life, perish by fire, in Jesus name.

(6) Father, let the blood of Jesus purchase back any of my property in the custody of the enemy, in Jesus name.

(7) Father, I touch the hem of your garment and I command every physical and spiritual problem in my life, to end now, in Jesus name.

(8) Father, every uniform of prisoner or slave I have been wearing, I pull it off and set it on fire, in Jesus name.

(9) Father, let any man or woman manipulating my life with evil power, fall down and die, in Jesus name.

(10) My Father my father, let any person tampering with my business, marriage, family, and finance, die by fire in Jesus name.

(11) Father, let any elected witch or wizard assigned to destroy me, receive fire and die by fire, in Jesus name.

(12) Father, let every satanic tailor authorized to sew an evil garment for me, receive fire and die by fire, in Jesus name.

(13) Father, cover me with your garment of righteousness, in Jesus name.

(14) Father, let every garment of shame, reproach, and disgrace, I have been wearing for years, catch fire, in Jesus name.

(15) Father, every fashion of this world that will make me miss heaven, please deliver me now, in Jesus name.

(16) Father, let every inherited garment that has brought a curse upon my life; receive fire, in Jesus name.

(17) Father, every garment of madness presented to me by the enemy, I reject it, in the name of Jesus.

(18) Father, decorate my life with the garment of favor so that my life will attract favor from God and man, in Jesus name.

(19) My Father my maker, let every satanic spy, monitoring me wherever I go, receive fire from heaven and die, in Jesus name.

(20) God of Elijah, arise by fire and consume every satanic cloth in my wardrobe, in Jesus name.

DAY FIFTEEN

LEAVE THAT CURSED LAND

Text: II King 2:18-22

Thunder Quote: (The history of a cursed land gives the secret about the place.)

Where you live and where you grew up matters a lot. Apart from friends, the environment is another factor that can also determine a man's destiny. Lands have been in existence for many years. It is among the things that God created. It is a pity that so many problems affecting people are traced to the bad and corrupt environment. A corrupt land will always have corrupt people living there. Lot made a mistake by living and raising up his children in Sodom and Gomorrah; a land full of sins and immoralities. If you grow up in a cursed land, the curse of that land may affect your destiny. Jericho was cursed by Joshua in Joshua 6:26, "And Joshua adjured them at the time, saying, cursed be the man before the LORD, that riseth up and buildeth this city Jericho: he shall lay the foundation, and in his youngest son shall he set up the gates of it." The curse Joshua pronounced upon the land of Jericho affected the land and its habitats, to the extent that the land was barren and people were dying, thank God for using Elisha to reverse the curse. I don't think Elisha would have been able to reverse the curse without contacting the double portion of Elijah's anointing. You need an extraordinary power to break any ancient curse. Have you ever asked yourself, why it was difficult for the fifty sons of the Prophets in the land of Jericho to break the curse of their land?

Psalm 11:3 says, "If the foundation is destroyed, what can the righteous do?" There are so many righteous people living in a cursed land, it is not that they will die, but they won't experience progress because the land is cursed.

Many people are ignorant of the environment they found themselves. I was sent to start a Church in a particular area in Lagos; I made a research about the place and discovered that Churches doesn't strive in the environment because most of the people in the land are Idol Worshippers and Muslim, only the no indigene and tenants are Christians. Any Church that comes to the land doesn't stay up to six months before it will pack up; we stayed over three years before relocating to a better place. Listen, there are environmental powers operating in most lands, claiming ownership, there is also environmental demons and strongman assigned to monitor most places. The day you move into their environment, they are aware because that is their domain. In the book of Daniel 10, there was a principality called the prince of the Kingdom of Persia that hindered the prayer of Daniel for twenty-one days. Please note, in every land, there is a god in charge of the land that you must bind and defeat if you want to possess the land so that you don't end up being possessed. A cursed land can truncate a man's destiny. The curse is very powerful. In Genesis Chapter four, after God cursed Cain for killing his brother Abel in verse eleven, "And art thou cursed from the earth, which hath opened her mouth to receive thy brother's blood from thy hand." Due to the curse pronounced upon him, he lamented in verse thirteen "And Cain said unto the LORD, my punishment is greater than I can bear" Are you under any divine curse? Please go to God in the prayer of mercy, because if you are under a divine curse, and you are living in a cursed environment, life will be hell on earth. May that never be your portion, in Jesus name. In Ruth 1:1-7, a man called Elimelech relocated his family, unknown to him to a cursed land called Moab, he died in the land and his two sons that got married ten years after his death also died, his wife Naomi ended up a widow and his sons wives also became widows, what a sad story. I pray for you reading this book; may God take you away from any land that takes people's lives, in Jesus name. May God direct you to the right place as long as you live. In Genesis 19:28-38, Lot foolishly resides in Sodom and Gomorrah, his two daughters ended up committing an abomination with him by having sex with him. Moab was the son of Lot, which one of his daughters gave birth to him, it is a country lay east of the Dead Sea, it is not a good place to dwell because it is too corrupt, it is also an idolatrous country that worships Chemosh, god of the Moabite. The foundation of Moab was faulty. Until Ruth relocated from Moab, she would have died a nobody, she is one of the progenitors of our Lord Jesus. The history of a cursed land gives the secret about the place. Please always make research before searching. A particular brother that was very close to me, got married and decided to live in an area he didn't make any research or inquired from God about, unknowing to him the house was cursed because most of the tenants occupying the house have lost at least one member of their family. Miscarriage is the order of the day in his marriage, the last pregnancy the wife had, she almost died before they relocated out of the house, eventually, the wife gave birth after some weeks when they left the house, glory blood. Another brother moves into a flat in Lagos with his wife that was pregnant, and his brand new car, in the same house, the wife died, his car got burnt and he left the house empty. Someone came to share the experience he had in his formal place, he said, ever since he moved into the house, the same money he made before he rented the flat has been the same money he has been spending, and after the money got finished, no money ever came to his hand despite series of miscarriage the wife had gone through. After a night vigil in their house, the wife conceive and gave birth to a bouncing baby boy, his business also experienced a turn around after they left the house. You are the next person to testify, in Jesus name.

PRAYER BOMB

(1) Father, I thank you for taking me out of every cursed land, house, and environment, in Jesus name.

(2) Father, let every ancient curse upon the land I found myself, break by fire, in Jesus name.

(3) Father, every land or house of bondage I found myself, take me out by fire, in Jesus name.

(4) Every strong man or strong woman having right over the affairs of my life, I bind you and cast you out, in Jesus name.

(5) Every territorial strong man and environmental powers, attacking me, receive fire from heaven and scatter, in Jesus name.

(6) Holy Ghost fire, locate any shrine or altar existing in the land; I dwell, in Jesus name.

(7) My Father, my maker, let every principality and power from my neighborhood monitoring me about, fail in their mission, in Jesus name.

(8) Father, let every satanic meeting organized by forces of darkness because of me, scatter by fire, in Jesus name.

(9) Father, any sinful land that wants me to land in hell after leaving this world, I fly out from it by fire, in Jesus name.

(10) Father, let every bareness upon the land I live affecting me from being productive; receive the anointing of fruitfulness in Jesus name.

(11) Father, send me help from above against forces of darkness in my territory, in Jesus name.

(12) Father, every man made of gold reigning over my life, bow to Jesus, in Jesus name.

(13) Father, every satanic land that takes people's life, relocate me from it by fire by force, in Jesus name.

(14) Every spirit of oppression and depression operating in my neighborhood, I bind and cast you out, in Jesus name.

(15) My Father my maker, let every satanic mission of the enemy against the plan of God concerning me, scatter by fire, in Jesus name.

(16) Father, please order my steps in every step I take in life so that I won't end up in regret, in Jesus name.

(17) God of Elijah, visit every satanic camp of the enemies constructed in my neighborhood by fire, in Jesus name.

(18) Thunder and earthquake from heaven, locate every head of witches and wizards in my community now, in Jesus name.

(19) Father, let every house of bondage housing my blessing, collapse by fire and release my blessing, in Jesus name.

(20) Father, I take authority over every power of darkness in my community from today, in Jesus name.

DAY SIXTEEN

ONLY THE VIOLENT CAN TAKE IT BY FORCE

Text: Genesis 32:24-30

Thunder Quote: (Violent is the only language the devil understands.)

Life is an arena of the battle for those that are ready to fight. If you are not prepared to fight, you may end up dead in the battle. Matthew 11:12 says, "And from the days of John the Baptist until now the Kingdom of heaven suffered violence, and the violent take it by force." If you are not violent, you can't take what belongs to you from the hand of the enemy. In Revelation 12:7-8 the Bible says, "And there was war in heaven: Michael and his angel fought against the dragon, and the dragon fought and his angels, And prevailed not, neither was their place found any more in heaven." Angel Michael had to be violent with other angels in other to prevail against the devil. Many people act like gentle men in the battle field, no wonder they end up dead. The devil is not a gentle man, that's why you must be violent. Violence is the only language the devil understands.

Violence from the Oxford advanced learner's dictionary means, involving or caused by a physical force that is intending to hurt or kill somebody. According to our text, Jacob wrestled with an angel until the hollow of the thigh was out of joint, at the end, he got his miracle. I have often said that life is no retreat, no surrender for those that desire victory. You don't give up or quit in the war front, you keep fighting until you win, and when you've won, you keep winning until you become a winner. If you desire victory in life, you must be ready to take the risk. In the book of Esther 4:15-17, Queen Esther, decided to risk her life for sake of her people, she said, "If I perish, I perish" The risk she took brought favor to her, instead of a death sentence. Late Benson Idahosa of blessed memory, in one of his message, says, "there is no limitation on what you want to be if you can give it what it takes." Without determination, the destination is not guaranteed. In the book of Daniel Chapter three, Shadrach, Meshach, and Abednego refused to commit idolatry by bowing to a man-made god apart from their own God, the Almighty, and when they were threatened to renounce their God or to be thrown into the burning fiery furnace, they became violent in one accord in Daniel 3:16-18, that they are not careful not to answer the king in the matter, that their God will deliver them. Daniel 11:32 says, "But the people that do know their God shall be strong, and do exploit." May the Almighty God give you the boldness and courage to face your enemy from today, in Jesus name.

Greatness is an issue of the mind, and not of the mouth, if you are not ready to be violent, greatness will only end up in your lips. In Mark 5:24-34, the woman with the issue of blood was violent and desperate to get her miracle despite the multitude blocking her focus from touching the hem of Jesus garment. She travails violently and prevails in getting her miracle by fire by force, and her continuous menstruation issue that has defied solution for 12 years, miraculously became a history and history within 24hours. I don't know how long or how old you have dwelled in that disgrace problem; I speak an end to it now, in Jesus name! The God that put a permanent stop to the case of the woman with the issue of blood, will put a permanent stop to that problem embarrassing you before your fellow human being, in Jesus name! Blind Bartimaeus in Mark 10:46, got his sight back because he was violent, he ignored the embarrassment he encountered from the crowd when they told him to shut up, he became angry and cried out violently and he got the attention of Jesus and the same people that asked him to shut up, told him, he calleth thee, and he received his sight. I pray for you, anyone oppressing your life will be a disgrace, in the name of Jesus. Don't close your mouth if anybody is asking you to close your mouth, remember a mouth closed is a closed destiny.

Rachel became violent to her husband when she discovered that she was going childless in Genesis 30:1, she said, "Give me children or I die." At last, God gave her Joseph that became a Prime Minister in a foreign land. May the Almighty God give you a miracle that will announce you to the whole world, in Jesus name. Lastly, in 1Chronicles 4:9-10, talks about Jabez, he became violent to his shameful situation and cried out to his God in verse ten "Oh that thou wouldest bless me indeed, and enlarge my coast and that thine hand might be with me and thou wouldest keep me from evil that it may not grieve me. And God granted him that which he requested." I decree in the name of Jesus, none of your prayers will fall to the ground in this spiritual exercise in Jesus name! You will reap answers to your prayers in form of blessings, testimonies, breakthroughs, and miracles, in Jesus name.

Only a coward flees when he sees war. Margret Thatcher says, "sometimes to win a battle, you need to fight it more than once." Receive strength from above to win in every battle of your life, in Jesus name.

PRAYER BOMB

(1) Father, I thank you for divine empowerment, to be violence to get my miracle by force by force, in Jesus name.

(2) Father, I receive power from above to become violent against every stubborn enemy, in Jesus name.

(3) Holy Ghost fire, enter my life and make me a terror to the kingdom of darkness, in Jesus name.

(4) My Father my maker, by fire by force, I collect back anything and everything the enemy has forcefully collected from me, in Jesus name.

(5) God of Elijah, turn me into a flame of fire, to dismantle and destroy every power of darkness surrounding my life, in Jesus name.

(6) Father, let every household enemy and unfriendly friend having a say over my life, receive divine judgment and die, in Jesus name.

(7) Holy Ghost fire, enter my destiny and reverse ever irreversible storm terrorizing my life, in Jesus name.

(8) Father, I receive the spirit of boldness and courage to face every enemy against my life, in Jesus name.

(9) Father, I speak an instant end to every problem that is making me hide from my mates, in Jesus name.

(10) Father, every long time war between me and reproach, come to an end by fire, in Jesus name.

(11) Father, put a permanent end to every disgracing problem in my life, in Jesus name.

(12) Father, let every satanic robber stealing my blessing unknowingly to me, receive fire and die by fire, in Jesus name.

(13) Father, let every man or woman giving information about me to the enemy, fall down and die, in Jesus name.

(14) Lord of Host, this battle is too hard for me, please arise in your anger and fight for me, in Jesus name.

(15) In the name of Jesus, I cancel every evil name affecting my life from excelling, in Jesus name.

(16) Father, let every limitation or barrier against my progress in life, scatter by fire, in Jesus name.

(17) Father, turn me into a battle axe, to uproot and pull down every satanic plantation growing in my life, in Jesus name.

(18) My Father, my creator, let your presence go ahead of me now and slaughter every enemy of my progress, in Jesus name.

(19) Father, give me a miracle that will announce me to the whole world, in Jesus name.

(20) Father, laminate my life with the fire of the Holy Ghost to become untouchable and unkillable, in Jesus name.

DAY SEVENTEEN

NO RETREAT, NO SURRENDER

Text: 1Samuel 17:32-37, 49-51

Thunder Quote: (Don't retire, but refire until you acquire what you desire.)

As long as you are still living in this world, you are on the battle field. Life is full of battle, that is the reason why every new born baby cries the moment they are born into this world. No retreat means no withdraw after a defeat or no withdraw from an uncomfortable situation or no moving back. No retreat no surrender is mainly used in the military to charge the soldiers to fight more.

No surrender means, no submit to superior force or give up to a superior power. Matthew 11:12 says, "And from the days of John the Baptist until now the Kingdom of heaven suffereth violence and the violent take it by force." If you are not violent prayer man, you can't win in the battle of life. There is no body in the world that is not fighting at least a battle; some are fighting the marital battle, financial battle, family battle, academical battle, spiritual battle, health battle and ministerial battle.

It is either you are the one fighting or God is fighting on your behalf. By strength shall no man prevail, not by power nor by might but by my spirit says the Lord. Any battle you fight by yourself, it is certain you will never win, but when you hand over the battle to God, victory is sure. In Exodus 14:14, the Bible says,

"The LORD shall fight for you, and ye shall hold your peace." Many people fail to invite God into their battle and they end up a loser. No soldier goes to war front without proper training. God will not allow you go into any battle without preparing you. You can't win a battle you are not prepared for. In Revelation 12:7-8, the Bible says "And there was war in heaven: Michael and his angels fought against the dragon, and the dragon fought and his angels, And Prevailed not, neither was their place found any more in heaven."

Michael and his angels were trained by God for war, which was the reason why they were able to defeat the dragon (devil).

David was able to kill the bear, lion and finally killed Goliath because he had gone through divine training. The major difference between civilians and soldiers are; soldiers are mainly trained for war, they don't easily give up like a civilian. A man who complains is already defeated. A man is not finished when he is defeated; it is when he quit while fighting. Victors never quit. In life, you need to fight some battles more than once to be a winner. Don't retire, but refire until you acquire what you desire. If you fight and run away, you will need to fight again until you win. No pain, no gain, no cross, no glory. If you are defeated in any battle, don't just lie down on the floor, stand up and try again. Because you failed yesterday, it doesn't mean you will fail today. Don't allow yesterday's failure to affect today's success, yesterday is gone, plan for today. Winners are ex-losers who got angry with their situation. Micah 7:8 says, "Rejoice not against me, O mine enemy, when I fall, I shall arise again."Anytime you fall, rise up, never surrender to the enemy, It is dangerous, because you may end up dead. In 1Samuel 17, the moment David prevailed against Goliath, Goliath fell down and it was an opportunity for David to behead him.

It is either you surrender and the enemy wins, or you win and the enemy surrender, remember the only person you are supposed to surrender to is Jesus Christ. David was bold to face Goliath because God had given him victory on so many occasions, he had killed a bear and a lion and he had confidence in the God that gave victory. It is not the size of the enemy that matters but the size of your God, 1John 4:4 says, "Ye are of God, little children, and have overcome them: because greater is he that is in you than he that is in the world." When you are bold and courageous, you can't retreat or surrender. The Bible says, in Proverbs 28:1, "The wicked flee when no man pursueth: but the righteous are as bold as lion." If the Lion of the tribe of Judah dwells in you, victory is certain. From now hence forth, your enemies will be afraid whenever they see you, in Jesus name.

PRAYER BOMB

(1) Father, I thank you for the grace of not to retreat or surrender in the battle of life you granted me, in Jesus name.
(2) Father, empower me so that I can have the power to fight and win in every battle of life, in Jesus name.
(3) Father, I command every spirit of fear occupying my life, to get out by fire, in Jesus name.
(4) Holy Ghost fire, I partner with you, consume to ashes every intimidator of my destiny, in Jesus name.
(5) Lion of the tribe of Judah, please be by my side in every battle, so that I can be victorious, in Jesus name.

(6) Father, I surrender and hand over my life to you, please fight for me, in Jesus name.

(7) Every Goliath troubling my life, I behead you now, die by the sword of fire, in Jesus name.

(8) Family Goliath boasting against my destiny, I behead you with the sword of fire, in Jesus name.

(9) Powers that want to turn me to widow/widower overnight, die by the sword of fire, in Jesus name.

(10) This year shall not swallow me and any members of my family, in Jesus name.

(11) This year, hear the word of the Lord, vomit my prosperity, in Jesus name.

(12) Roundabout battles in my life, hear the word of the Lord, go into captivity, in Jesus name.

(13) Dream battles in my life, die by the sword of fire, in Jesus name.

(14) Family battles in my life, die by the sword of fire, in Jesus name.

(15) Association of wicked elders in my environment, fighting against my prosperity, scatter by fire, in Jesus name.

(16) Thou power showing me coffin in my dream, enter into your coffin, in Jesus name.

(17) I am a winner and not a loser! I am more than a conqueror, in Jesus name.

(18) Father let every gang up of the enemy holding evil meeting anywhere to attack me, receive fire and die, in Jesus name.

(19) Lord of Host, I hand over every battle that is stronger than me to you take over, in Jesus name.

(20) Thank you, Jesus, for giving me victory, in Jesus name.

DAY EIGHTEEN

LIBERATED FROM THE POWER OF POVERTY

Text: 1king 17:8-15

Thunder Quote: (It is the truth that you know that can set you free.)

The day I read a book titled, "Poverty is too expensive, I can't afford it." My mindset changed from that day and I told myself, I refuse to be poor. Poverty is a choice, prosperity is a choice. The choice you make in life is very important.

There are powers behind poverty that is the reason why you need to be liberated from poverty. According to our topic, Liberated from the Power of Poverty, we have three vital words: liberated, power and poverty. Let me defined them one after the other.

(1) Liberated: It means to set someone free. In John 8:36, the Bible stated clearly that, if the Son, therefore, shall make you free, ye shall be free indeed. Also in John 8:32, the Bible says, "And ye shall know the truth, and the truth shall make you free." Jesus is the truth according to John 14:6, it is the truth that you know that can set you free. For you to be free, you must know the truth, and the best way to know him is by digging deep into his word. Jesus is the only one that can set the captives free, In Isaiah 49:24-25; "Shall the prey be taking from the mighty or shall the lawful captive delivered?" But thus saith the Lord, even the captives of the mighty shall be taken away and the

prey of the terrible shall be delivered: for I will contend with him that contendeth with thee, and I will save their children." For a reader of this book, where they have detained you all these years, receive freedom now, in Jesus name! I set your glory, star, destiny, business, marriage, family and finance free from every satanic warehouse, in Jesus name.

(2) Power: Means the ability to do something. Psalm 62:11 says, power belongs to God. There is a power that comes from God and there is also the power that comes from the devil, but all power belongs to God. In Act 1:8a, the Bible says, "But ye shall receive power, after that the Holy Ghost is come upon you, that kind of power is from God." If you look at the book of Luke 4:6, "And the devil said unto him, All this power will I give thee, and the glory of them: for that is delivered unto me; and whosoever will I give it." Please note that, after God chased Lucifer from heaven, he was driven to the world and became the god of the world. For you to be liberated from the power of poverty, you need a higher power from above.

(3) Poverty: It means the state of being poor, lack of human necessity. Poverty is a stranger or an enemy that brings disgrace to its victim. Don't romance or embrace poverty, give poverty quite notice and say no to poverty. You must change your poverty mindset to prosperity mindset. Romans 12:2says, "Be ye transform by the renewal of your mind." If your thinking is right, you will act well, as a man thinketh in his heart, so is he, Pro 23:7. It is your covenant right to prosper according to 111John 2. It is programmed in the plan of God that you will prosper if you can believe. God didn't put your name in

Deuteronomy 15:11, "for the poor shall never cease out the land." As a bonafide child of God, it is already a settled matter, that you will be rich, how can the son of a King live in poverty. The Bible says Jesus became poor so that through his poverty you can be prosperous. I speak prosperity into your destiny from today; you will never experience anything called poverty again! I decree into every ramification of your life; bye to poverty, and welcome to prosperity, in Jesus name. That power behind poverty motivating you to steal, go into prostitution, do ritual money or kill yourself, I destroy that power now, in Jesus name. Poverty will not end your life, you will not die in poverty, that pit of poverty that has swallowed you will vomit you, in the land of prosperity. I decree from today, your prosperity has begun, before you die, the world will hear about you.

Poverty has turned many men into gentle men, naturally, they are not gentle, but due to poverty, they can't talk where their mates are talking. Some people can't make a decision or contribute in their family meeting because of poverty. From today, no meeting will hold in that your family without your presence. Money that answereth all things will answer for you in the time of need. Those that thought you will die in poverty, will see you live in prosperity, your account will move from local to a foreign account, God will turn you into a bank of money that lend to the nation, in Jesus name.

7 Ways you can be Liberated from the Power of Poverty

(1) Receive Jesus into your life. John 1:12

(2) Remember God after you have been liberated - Duet 8:18

(3) Be diligent – Pro. 22:29

(4) Pay your Tithe – Mal 3:10

(5) Give – Luke 6:38

(6) Hate Sleep - Pro. 20:13

(7) Study & Meditate the word – Josh 1:8.

PRAYER BOMB

(1) Father, I thank you for liberating me from the power of Poverty, in Jesus name.
(2) Holy Ghost fire, chase away every spirit of Poverty occupying my life, in Jesus name.
(3) Father, I will not die in Poverty, I will live in Prosperity before I die, in Jesus name.
(4) My destiny, reject Poverty from today, I am mandated to prosper, in Jesus name.
(5) Every power behind Poverty, I render you powerless over my life in Jesus name.
(6) Father, I receive divine speed to be faster than my mates in every area of life, in Jesus name.
(7) Father, I receive power from above to make money in my business and career, in Jesus name.
(8) My Father, my maker, let every power of darkness manipulating my destiny not to prosper, receive the fire of the Holy Ghost and scatter, in Jesus name.
(9) Father, please help me to become a wealthy man in my generation, in the name of Jesus.

(10) Father, I delete my name from any file containing poor people in my generation, in Jesus name.

(11) Oh Lord my God, open a permanent door of prosperity in my life, in Jesus name.

(12) My Father my maker, I have suffered enough in this life, please turn my suffering to enjoyment, in Jesus name.

(13) Father, any pit of Poverty that has swallowed me, vomit me now, in the land of prosperity in Jesus name.

(14) Father, let divine favor that turns poverty to prosperity locate me now, in Jesus name.

(15) Father, every satanic short cut to prosperity that shortens life, I reject it, in Jesus name.

(16) Father, please don't let me beg or borrow before I survive, in Jesus name.

(17) My Bank Account, receive the anointing from above and move to the next level, in Jesus name.

(18) Money that answers all thing in life, locate me now, in Jesus name.

(19) Father help me not to be under-control of money but to be in-control of money, when you have made me great, in Jesus name.

(20) Father, before I die, I shall spend my days in prosperity and my years in pleasures, in Jesus name.

DAY NINETEEN

CONFRONTING THAT MOUNTAIN WITH YOUR FAITH

Text: Joshua 6:1-5, 20

Thunder Quote: (Any mountain that you can't confront will consume you.)

The verb confronts from Oxford Advance Learner's Dictionary means:

(i) To deal with a problem or difficult situation.
(ii) To face somebody so that they cannot avoid seeing or hearing you.
(iii) To deal with an unpleasant or difficult person or situation.
(iv) To have something in front of you that has to deal with or react to.

On the other hand, the mountain is a very high hill, often with rocks near the top or high elevation of the earth. Faith is confidence in the testimony of another. Considering the fourth meaning of the verb confront; to have something in front of you that you have to deal with or react to. The wall of Jericho is likening to a mountain the children of Israel needs faith to confront. You need faith to confront any problem in this world, whether physical or spiritual, visible or invisible. Faith is the visa to breakthrough. In four different part in the Bible, God says, the just shall live by faith: Romans 1:17, Habakkuk 2:4b, Galatians 3:11b and Hebrews 10:38a.

The children of Israel believed God and his servant Joshua when they confronted the wall of Jericho by faith, they shouted Halleluyah seven times and the wall of Jericho fell down flat. As you shot seven Halleluyah now, every wall of Jericho or mountain before you and your miracle will fall down flat, in Jesus name! Shout Halleluyah. Halleluyah means praise ye the Lord. When a problem, like poverty, sickness, failure or bareness hears Hallelujah, they bow and crumble. That mountain problem in your life will bow and crumble today, in Jesus name. In Matthew 17:20, the Bible says, And Jesus said unto them, because of your unbelief: for verily I say unto you, If ye have faith as a grain of mustard seed, ye shall say unto the mountain, remove hence to yonder place and it shall remove, and nothing shall be impossible unto you." In Hebrews 11:6, it says, "But without faith, it is impossible to please Him." Before you confront any mountain, make sure you have faith, so that the mountain doesn't collapse on you. It is either you confront that mountain with faith and its collapse than to run from it and it collapses on you.

In 1Samuel 17, Goliath was a mountain in the sight of King Saul and the children of Israel, but David saw Goliath as an opportunity to the top. In Numbers 13, Moses sent spies to search the land of Canaan, they all saw giants, some came with the evil report because of the giants, Joshua and Caleb saw the giants as an opportunity to possess the land. If David had run away from Goliath, he wouldn't have become a King. The righteous are as bold as a lion, Pro 28:1b. Boldness, courage, and determination will help you to confront any mountain. In 1Sam 17:45 "Then said David said to the Philistine, Thou comest to me with a sword, and with a spear, and with a shield; but I come to thee in the name of the Lord of Host, the God of the armies of Israel." You can't confront mountains with physical weapons, the spiritual controls physical. For you to pull down the mountain, you must apply Spiritual weapon. The weapon of our warfare is not carnal, not a physical weapon but strong to the pulling down stronghold. The Lord of Host is the mighty man in battle, the only one who can never be defeated. Who you call, or run to in the time of trouble determines whether you will be victorious or defeated. Proverbs 18:10 says, "the name of the Lord is a strong tower, the righteous runneth into it, and was safe." Faith is a weapon of warfare, without faith, your miracle will end up being a mirage. Without faith, you won't reach your destination.

MOUNTAINS TO CONFRONT WITH YOUR FAITH

(1) Mountain of Doubt/Fear: Doubt and fear are twin brothers, which can alter a man's destiny. Doubt brings fear into the life of a man, and fear is the opposite of faith. Without faith, there is nothing you ask from God that you will receive. God has not given us the spirit of fear, but power and love and of a sound mind. Receive divine boldness to confront every physical and spiritual mountain, in Jesus name.

(2) Mountain of Failure: In Luke 5:1-7, Peter was a professional fisherman that went fishing at the right time, right tools and caught nothing. He failed at that day and decided to wash his net when Jesus stepped into his case and asked him to try again; he tried and broke the record in fishing that day. A

failure is an event, that fact you failed doesn't make you a failure.

(3) **Mountain of Poverty:** Many are confronted with this mountain and end up being a victim due to ignorance of the word of God. Poverty is a choice; failure to pay the price out of poverty will keep a man inside poverty. A lot of people are poor today because they fail to pay the price of prosperity. Poverty is worst than cancer disease, refuse to be poor because you are not created to be poor.

(4) **Mountain of Generation Curse:** Mountain of generation curse is affecting many individual today, due to what their fathers and fore fathers had done in the past. In 11kings 5:27, Gehazi brought leprosy upon his unborn generation because of greed. Lamentation 5:7, says, "our fathers have sinned, and are not and we have borne their iniquities."

(5) **Mountain of Sickness:** Anyone confronted with this kind of mountain can only survive by the grace and mercy of God because only a few have faith to bounce back again. When your faith fails, it only takes the mercy of God to restore you back. You need great faith to confront this kind of mountain.

(6) **Mountain of Household Enemy:** A man's greatest enemy is members of the household; these are people that know almost everything about your history. Joseph experienced that kind of mountain in his family due to his great dream he told his

brethren, they conspired against him to kill him and later sold him as a slave in Gen 37:18-28.

(7) Mountain of Delay: This Mountain can stagnate a man in a particular place, or position for a long period of time unless there is divine intervention. For example delay in having children, delay in getting married. The man in John 5:1-9 experience 38 years delay of healing before he was healed.

PRAYER BOMB

(1) Power of God overshadows my life, in Jesus name.
(2) O God, arise and discharge and acquit me from any satanic accusation, in the name of Jesus.
(3) Mountains of the problem in my life, vanished, in Jesus name.
(4) Mountain of doubt and fear in my life crumble, in Jesus name.
(5) Mountain of failure in my life, crumble by fire, in Jesus name.
(6) Mountain of poverty in my life, be uprooted in Jesus name.
(7) Mountain of the generational curse in my life, receive thunder fire and scatter, in Jesus name.
(8) Mountain of sickness, hear the word of the Lord, crumble from your foundation, in Jesus name.
(9) Mountains of the household enemy in my life crumble by fire, in Jesus name.
(10) Mountain of delay in my life receive the sword of fire and crumble, in Jesus name.
(11) I lose myself from every inherited mountain, in Jesus name.

(12) Every Herod standing as mountain against my life, die right now, in Jesus name.
(13) Power saying I will not go far in life, be crushed into pieces, in Jesus name.
(14) Mountain of chains upon my hands, break by fire, in Jesus name.
(15) Every stumbling block to my advancement, be roasted out, in Jesus name.
(16) Lord, baptized me with faith that will remove mountains, in Jesus name.
(17) Anything planted in my life as a mountain, to destroy my destiny, come out by fire, in Jesus name.
(18) The mountain of "almost there" in my life, die, in Jesus name.
(19) Evil Lion of past mountains roaring against me, shut up, in the name of Jesus.
(20) O Lord, prove your name in my situation, in Jesus name.

DAY TWENTY

POVERTY MUST LEAVE MY LIFE

Text: Judges 6:13-15

Thunder Quote: (Poverty always forces a man to look for a cheap alternative.)

Poverty is the situation or experience of being poor, it is also a state of lack, and lack comes as a result of the unavailability of money to get one's needs. Gideon came from a poor family and he is the least in the father's house according to Judges 6:15. Don't allow your family background to put you on the ground. The fact that your father is poor, doesn't mean you must be poor. Poverty is a spirit that can't be conquered by mere hard work, or else Africans would have become one of the richest set of people in the world because they are hard workers. The reflection of poverty shows in the home in the aspect of; poor education, shelter, dressings, state of health and quality of food. Lack of money according to an author is the root of all bitterness.

Poverty can lead its victims into destruction, for instance, poverty will make a man join armed robbery or kill his child for money ritual. Many have committed suicide simply because of lack of money to meet their needs. Poverty always forces a man to look for a cheaper alternative in life. Lack of money will make someone buy second-hand clothes instead of new ones. Lack of money will make one travel a far journey of 48 hours by road instead of traveling by air for an hour. A poor man goes to what is affordable and not what is available. A poor man doesn't have a choice. To be poor and to be prosperous in life is a matter of choice.

5 THINGS THAT CAN TURN YOU INTO A POOR MAN

(1) Laziness: proverb 22:29 "Seest thou a man diligent in his business? He shall stand before the king; he shall not stand before mean man." God can never bless a lazy man. Many people take prayer serious but despise working hard. God open doors when you pray but diligence takes you through the door into your blessing. A diligent person works hard, people who are not diligent end up in poverty. Hard work is part of life, even God worked. He who refuses hard work, life will be hard for him. Proverb 24:33-34. May God baptize you with the spirit of diligent, in Jesus name.

(2) Stinginess: A stingy is the person that is not generous, someone that doesn't give willingly. Proverbs 11:24 says," There is that scattered and yet in increaseth, and there is that withholdeth more than is meet, but tendeth to poverty" God's principle of prosperity start with giving. If you withhold from God, your blessing will be withheld from you. Anything you give to return to you in several folds.

(3) Ignorance: Hosea 4:6 "My people are destroyed for lack of knowledge." Ignorance is a silent killer that can destroy a man, the absence of information is ignorance, because when you are not informed, you will be deformed. A Christian could be poor

if he lacks the knowledge of God promise for him in the word of God. The word of God is the information that we need to turn our world around. God has the world for every man and his needs, his word can create our needs. It takes knowledge in the word of God to cancel poverty and move into the realm of prosperity. Even a man in debt can be liberated through the knowledge of God's word that he knows. A mindset of poverty can only keep you in financial bondage. "And ye shall know the truth, and the truth shall make you free." John 8:32.

(4) Disobedience: Disobedience is when you rebel against recognized authority. It's a destiny destroyer. The Bible says for rebellion is a sin of witchcraft. 1 Samuel 15:23. Failure to pay your tithe is disobedience which attracts curses. Obedience to God's commands brings commendation, but disobedience to God's commands brings condemnation. Isaiah 1:19-20 says "If ye be willing and obedient, ye shall eat the good of the land: But if ye refuse and rebel, ye shall be devoured with the sword." Obedience is better than sacrifice.

(5) Unfaithfulness: Whoever is unfaithful will become unfruitful. When the fruitful prosper the unfaithful suffer losses. Proverbs 24:19 says, "confidence in an unfaithful man in time of trouble is like a broken tooth, and a foot out of joint." An unfaithful man misbehaves. Unfaithfulness will make a man experience rise and fall in life.

PRAYER BOMB

(1) Father, I thank you for eradicating poverty from my life, in Jesus name.

(2) Poverty you are a stranger in my life. I command you to leave by fire, in Jesus name.

(3) Every spirit of lack of achievement manifesting in my life; come out now by fire, in Jesus name.

(4) Father, change poverty to prosperity in my life, in Jesus name.

(5) Every spirit of begging and borrowing to survive, leave my life now, in Jesus name.

(6) Father, let your light of prosperity shine upon me, in Jesus name.

(7) Father Lord, let every generational curse that has brought poverty into my life; be broken now, in Jesus name.

(8) Father, let every satanic bank holding my money, receive fire and release my money now, in Jesus name.

(9) Father, give me an excellent spirit to excel above all my mate in business, in Jesus name.

(10) Father, every connection I have with poverty, I break it by fire, in Jesus name.

(11) Father, deliver me from every bondage of poverty, in Jesus name.

(12) Every yoke of retrogression or backwardness placed upon me, be broken by fire, in Jesus name.

(13) Father, let every garment of poverty the enemy has forced upon me, catch fire, in Jesus name.

(14) My Father my Father, open the door of favor, success, and profit into my life, in Jesus name.

(15) Every satanic chain binding my destiny from moving forward, break by fire, in Jesus name.
(16) Father, let every power that wants me poor by all means, leave my life, in Jesus name.
(17) Father, I speak progress and elevation into my destiny, in Jesus name.
(18) Father, every spirit of idleness in my life, come out by fire, in Jesus name.
(19) Every evil eye from the kingdom of darkness upon my finance, I pluck you out by fire, in Jesus name.
(20) Father, give me the power to make money, in Jesus name.

DAY TWENTY-ONE

PRAY YOUR WAY OUT OF THAT PROBLEM

Text: I Chronicle 4:9-10

Thunder Quote: (Lack of prayer, increase and multiplies problems.)

Prayer is the key solution to any problem of life. Many people are ignorant of the power of prayer. Jabez was a man that discovered the importance of prayer, he prayed until he got his miracle. Besides, his problem started from his birth because his arrival into the world brought sorrow to his mother, and his mother decided to name him Jabez. One day Jabez realized that he needs to cry to his maker, or else he will end up being a nonentity, he cried violently and the Bible confirmed that God granted him that which he requested. "The effectual fervent prayer of a righteous man availeth much."-James 5:16. There is nobody existing in this world without a problem.

Problems are part of the things we must encounter as a living being, as our faces are different, so our problems. You must be ready and prepare because anything can happen to you in life. Anybody without a problem is a problem to the world, the Bible says, in this world, we shall pass through divers tribulations. It is the only prayer that can eradicate, or alter problems when it arises, that is why God says watch and pray less ye enter into diverse temptations. Prayer is a solution to any problem. Mark 11:24 says, "Therefore I say unto you, what thing so ever ye desire, when ye pray, believe that ye receive them, and ye shall have them."

Complaining, murmuring and crying doesn't change any problem. Job 22:27 says, "Thou shalt make thy prayer unto him, and he shall hear thee, and thou shalt pay thy vows." It is what you do to your problem when you don't do anything, nothing happens. Lack of prayer increase and multiplies the problem.

Jonah would have ended up dead in the belly of the fish, but he prayed his way out, and he came out, Jonah 2:1-2. Hannah prayed her way out of barrenness and became fruitful. Lack of prayer will make a man powerless and an easy prey to the enemy, lack of prayer will make a man stay too long in his problem. If you don't pray through, you won't breakthrough.

7 REASONS WHY PEOPLE STAY TOO LONG IN THEIR PROBLEM

(1) Laziness to pay Prices: Laziness in prayer will make a man spend so many years in a particular problem.
(2) Absent of Faith: Doubt and unbelief show that a man doesn't have faith, and without faith, there is no way a man can receive a solution to its problem. Many people don't have faith in their spiritual life. The Bible says, ''the just shall live by faith not by fear.''
(3) Bad Foundation: Psalm 11:3, says when the foundation laid is faulty; raising block on it is a waste.
(4) Procrastination: When you delay something that you should do, you will experience a delay.
(5) Sin: When you commit an offense against God's law, one will be chocked inside problems.

(6) Lack of Knowledge: Hosea 4:6. Knowledge is power.
(7) No Personal Relationship with God: You need God to survive in life, without God you are nothing. John 15:5c, "for without me ye can do nothing."

PRAYER BOMB

(1) Father, I thank you because I am coming out of every problem today, in Jesus name.
(2) My prayer life, receive fire from heaven and be ignited, in Jesus name.
(3) My Father my Father, let every power of darkness attacking my prayer life, scatter by fire, in Jesus name.
(4) Father, empower me to pray through into my breakthrough today, in Jesus name.
(5) Oh Lord my God, Jabez prayed, you answered him, Hannah also prayed and you answered her, please answer me by fire, in the name of Jesus.
(6) Father, let every problem that has stayed long in my life, expire now, in Jesus name.
(7) My Father, my maker, let every problem in my life, resisting solution all these years, come to an end, in Jesus name.
(8) Demons, principalities, and powers manufacturing problems into my life, stop your activities and leave my life, in Jesus name.
(9) Father, every foundational fault from my background that is affecting my destiny, I demolish it, in Jesus name.
(10) Father Lord, compliment anything that is making me complain about a complete miracle, in Jesus name.

(11) Every spirit of fear affecting my faith, you are in trouble, leave my life now, in Jesus name.

(12) Father, give me the solution to every problem affecting my destiny, in Jesus name.

(13) Your spirit of doubt and unbelief imposed upon my life, I bind you and me command you to leave my life now, in Jesus name.

(14) Father, any problem from the pit of hell attached to my life, be destroyed by fire, in Jesus name.

(15) My Father my maker, let every generational problem rotating in my lineage all these years, disappear by fire, in Jesus name.

(16) Consuming fire of the Holy Ghost, consume by fire all the problems that want to consume me, in Jesus name.

(17) Oh Lord my God, I have stayed long in this disgracing problem, please deliver me now, in Jesus name.

(18) Father Lord, let any problem in my life that is disgracing me before my mates, disappear now, in Jesus name.

(19) Father, in respect of the last statement you said on the cross of Calvary, I decree and declare my problem ends today, in Jesus name.

(20) Father, ignite my prayer life with fresh fire from above to become a prayerful vessel, in Jesus name.

DAY TWENTY-TWO

CONTACTING THE ANOINTING TO PRODUCE RESULT

Text: Luke 5:1-7

Thunder Quote: (When you don't have result in life, you will be insulted.)

In respect of our text, Peter went fishing with his colleagues as usual; he caught nothing after all night laboring. When morning came, he decided to wash his net, rest and prepare for another night of fishing, before Jesus came into his situation and turn his lack of result into an amazing miracle. Peter was an ordinary fisherman before he had an encounter with Jesus, the moment he contacted the anointing to produce a result, he became an extraordinary fisherman and was able to catch fishes he has never caught before in his life ever since he became a fisherman. I prophesy into that your business that is not bringing profit, from today, anointing from above will come upon it and you will begin to make an uncommon profit, in Jesus name.

Without the anointing, you can't have resulted in life because anointing makes the differences. When you lack the anointing, annoyance will manifest. Imagine a farmer that planted a mango seed and after some years, the mango tree refuses to produce mango, the farmer will never be happy. In business, everyone wants results, no result, no respect. When you lack the anointing, you will labor like the elephant in your business and reap like an ant. The insult comes in when you can't produce a result. I pray for you now, every insult you have received due to lack of result in your life shall turn to testimony, in Jesus name! In business, you either make profit or loss. I see you making a profit, in Jesus name. Also, in every examination, the result is more important, I see you coming out with flying colors in that examination, in Jesus name. You will never experience failure again, in Jesus name. That you failed doesn't make you a failure; tell yourself, I am a success!

As a man thinketh in his heart, so he is, Prov. 23:7. You are a product of your mindset, don't look down on yourself. No matter how educated you may be, if you lack visible result, nobody will celebrate you. Peter was a professional fisherman that went fishing at the right time, with the right people, with the right tools and caught nothing. The anointing has the power to break the yoke of lack of result in the life of a person. I decree in that name that is above every other name, every yoke of nothing to show forth in business, marriage, career, and life, I break it now, in your life! As from today, you will have something to show forth in Jesus name.

The anointing is a yoke breaker that has the ability to break the yokes. Isaiah 10:27 says, "And it shall come to the past in that day, that his burden shall be taken away from off thy shoulder, and his yoke from off thy neck, and the yoke shall be destroyed because of the anointing." I have no doubt, by the power, in the name of Jesus, that stubborn yoke is broken completely in your life. When you don't have result in life, you will be insulted. In 1Samuel Chapter one, Hannah was insulted because she doesn't have any result to show as a married woman. Right now, receive the anointing that turns insulted to result, in Jesus name!

HOW DO I CONTACT THE ANOINTING TO PRODUCE RESULT

(1) Surrender your life totally to God- John 1:12.

(2) Love righteousness and hate sin-Psalm 45:7.

(3) Desire and thirst for the anointing-Matt 5:6.

(4) Use your faith- Hebrew 11:6.

(5) Apply the A.S.K formula-Matt 7:7-8.

A - Ask

S – Seek

K – Knock

(6) Wait on the LORD– Isaiah 40:31.

(7) Give to a servant of God.

(8) Pray violently-Mk 11:24.

PRAYER BOMB

1. Father, I thank you for contacting the anointing to produce a result, in Jesus name.
2. Father, let every yoke of lack of result upon my destiny, break by fire, in Jesus name.

3. Cry out very loud and say "Anointing that break the yoke, fall upon me now and break every yoke in my life, in Jesus name.
4. God of Elijah, arise by fire and destroy every spirit of bad luck in my life, in Jesus name.
5. My Father my maker, turn every loss in life to profit, in Jesus name.
6. Every spirit compelling me to labor like an elephant and reap like an ant, get out of my life by fire, in Jesus name.
7. Every problem that has brought insults upon my life, catch fire and disappear, in Jesus name.
8. Every spirit of working hard without visible result, by fire by force, leave my life, in Jesus name.
9. My Father my maker, I need divine intervention concerning every problem, that is making people mock your name in my life, in Jesus name.
10. Father, I contact the anointing to excel above my entire mates, in Jesus name.
11. Lift up your two hands to heaven, and cry out violently "My hands, receive power from heaven to make money, in Jesus name.
12. Father, let every profitless effort programmed into my business; catch fire, in Jesus name.
13. Every generation curse of a failure affecting my life, break now, in Jesus name.
14. Every spirit of mere success syndrome and failure at the edge of success, leave my life, in the name of Jesus.
15. Holy Ghost fire, arise and chase out of my life every spirit of almost there, in Jesus name.
16. My Father, my maker, turn me into a result producer, in Jesus name.

17. Father, every mark of the tail and last, place upon my life, I wipe it off, in Jesus name.
18. Father, I command the power of failure having dominion over my life, to become powerless now, in Jesus name.
19. Every mouth in my family, place of work and neighborhood, on assignment to mock me, I shut you up permanently, in Jesus name.
20. Father, give me total victory over everyone and anyone that says, I won't amount to somebody in life, in Jesus name.

DAY TWENTY-THREE

MOVE FORWARD, DON'T MOVE BACKWARD

Text: Exodus 14:8-15

Thunder Quote: (When you move, God moves, when God moves, everything moves.)

According to science, the first characteristic of every living thing is movement. In life, it is either you are moving forward or backward, stagnation is not allowed. It is only living things that move, if you are not moving, you are not a living thing. You need the power to move forward in life. In our Bible text, Pharaoh and his men chased the children of Israel from the back, and when they noticed that the Egyptians were closed, they became afraid, in verse ten of our text, the Bible says, "And when Pharaoh drew nigh, the children of Israel lifted up their eyes, and behold, the Egyptians marched after them; and they were sore afraid, and the children of Israel cried out unto the LORD." I don't know the enemies chasing you from behind, God will give you divine speed, and they will not be able to catch up with you, in Jesus name.

Pharaoh was a stubborn enemy that don't want the children of Israel to move forward, who is that man or woman that says you will remain in that spot as long as he/she lives, may the ground open and swallow the person now, in Jesus name. The day the Israelite got their freedom, immediately the enemy began to chase them. When the children of Israel discovered that their enemies were closed, they were discouraged, to go back to Egypt to continue serving the Egyptians. Thank God for the bold leader they have that encouraged them, in spite of their fear. The Bible says in Exodus 14:13, "And Moses said unto the people, fear not, stand still, and see the salvation of the LORD, which he will show you today for the Egyptians whom ye have seen today, ye shall see them again no more forever." In verse thirty, the prophecy of Moses came to reality. I prophesy into your life, that Egyptians troubling your family, business, finance, marriage, and ministry, will perish and you will not see them anymore, in Jesus name.

Many people thought that they are moving forward in life, spiritually, the enemy has tied them up in one spot, they are only marching, and they are not moving. Moving forward is like taking a risk because; you don't know what await you in the front. In 11Kings 7:3-8, four lepers agreed to take a risk by leaving their comfort zone to move forward, verse three says "Why sit we here until die."

The moment they were determined to move forward, power came upon them from above and God turned their moment into the moment of noise of chariot, noise of horses and noise of great host that made the enemy left their camp with a lot of food that solve the famine in their land. From today, when the enemy discovered that you are coming, they will flee, in Jesus name. As a child of God, when you move, God moves, and when God moves everything move. The only way to move forward is by contacting the power to move.

When Elijah contact the power to move forward, he moved faster than Ahab that was on a chariot in 1Kings 18:46. David was an ordinary shepherd before he was anointed, the moment he contacted the power to move forward, he moved forward. The Bible told us in, 1Samuel 16:13, "Then Samuel took the horn of oil, and anointed him in the midst of his brethren: and the spirit of the LORD came upon David from that day forward." The opposite of forwarding is backward. Nothing move, until you move, you must take a step for God to step in. If you refuse to make a move, God won't make a move. Many people are stagnant because they refuse to move. If you don't move, you won't progress. Even the snail the slowest animal move to enter the ark with Noah.

In 1Samuel 30:1-19, when the Amalekite invaded Ziklag the camp of David, they took the family of David and his men including their goods, David and his men came to the camp it was empty, they started weeping until they have no more power to weep, but David encouraged himself in the LORD, he enquired from God, if he should pursue, and God told him to pursue, at the end, he recovered all that the enemy had taken from them. If you are discouraged you will be stagnated, but when you encourage yourself, you will move forward, overtake and recover. Receive grace from above to move from glory to glory and from victory to victory, in Jesus name.

PRAYER BOMB

(1) Father, I thank you for empowering me to move forward, in Jesus name.

(2) That strong man or strong woman refusing to let me go, fall down and die, in Jesus name.

(3) Father, I receive divine speed to move faster in life, in Jesus name.

(4) Father, let every enemy chasing me from the back, fall down and die, in Jesus name.

(5) All principalities and powers that have held me captives all these years, leave me and let me go, in Jesus name.

(6) Father, position me on the fast lane of a miracle so that I can move faster than all my mates, in Jesus name.

(7) Father, move me away from the back side of life to the front side, in Jesus name.

(8) Every arrow of starting and not finishing fired into my destiny, back to your sender, in Jesus name.

(9) My Father, my Father, let every power of backwardness and retrogression fighting against my progress in life, become powerless in Jesus name.

(10) Every satanic traffic programmed to limit my movement in life, clear by fire, in Jesus name.

(11) Father, move me to the level of nobody to somebody before I leave this world, in Jesus name.

(12) Every spirit or snail or tortoise cast into my destiny, receive fire and perish, in Jesus name.

(13) Father, let your grace cancel every disgracing problem in my life now in Jesus name.

(14) Every road blocker organized to slow me down on my way to the miraculous, scatter by fire, in Jesus name.

(15) Father, every yoke of the slow moment or go-slow upon my life is broken, in Jesus name.

(16) Father, every spirit of error directing me to the wrong places and wrong people, leave my life in Jesus name.

(17) Father, in the journey of success, I refuse to be the last, make me number one, in Jesus name.

(18) Father, let every pressure in my life, turn to pleasure, in Jesus name.

(19) Father, let every spirit of death assigned to take my life before completing my mission in this world, receive fire and leave my life, in Jesus name.

(20) Father, I receive divine speed to pursue, overtake and recover all my blessings in the hands of the enemy, in Jesus name.

DAY TWENTY-FOUR

PAY THE PRICE AND BE GREAT

Text: 1Kings 3:3-13

Thunder Quote: (If you can pay the price, you will get the prize.)

Solomon decided to pay the price or greatness and he became the greatest, wisest, famous and wealthiest in his generation. There is always a price to pay to get to the top, the ground floor is crowded, and there are vacancies on the top. King Solomon broke the record as long as giving is concerned, he provokes heaven and got divine attention. God gave him a blank cheque breakthrough because what he gave to God has never been given by anybody. When your gift exceeds the gift of others, you will experience open heaven. If you can pay the price, you will get the prize. God is the richest; he is even richer than the richest in the universe. Silver and gold belong to him according to Haggai 2:8. God desire for you is to prosper and be in health because health is wealth.

What is the purpose of being wealthy without being healthy? 111John 3 says, "Behold, I wish above all things that thou mayest prosper and be in health, even as thy soul prospereth." I decree prosperity into your destiny with effect from today, in Jesus mighty name! You will never experience lack again, in Jesus name. You may be asking yourself, does God want me to be rich? Yes, in Psalm 35:27, the Bible says, "Let the LORD be magnified, which hath pleasure in the prosperity of his servant." I guess God is happy when you prosper and he is not happy when you are poor. By the mandate of the TRINITY, every book containing poor people in your generation, I delete your name from it, in Jesus name. In Deut 8:18 says, "But thou shalt remember the LORD thy God for it is he that giveth the power to get wealth, that he may establish his covenant which he swears unto thy fathers, as it is this day." Do you know that as a bonafide child of God, there is a covenant of prosperity upon you that mandate you to prosper? Ignorance has robbed so many of their covenant right. Poverty has made so many people join the association of suffering and smiling. That spirit of poverty that is robbing you of your covenant right is eradicated from your life now, in Jesus name.

Some people now manage little earning to survive, the majority of people now eat what is available, and not what they want.By the power in the name of Jesus, I break that yoke of poverty in your life, receive power to make money and enjoy life to the fullness, in Jesus name. Hosea 4:6 says, "My people perish for lack of Knowledge." Knowledge is power, if you lack knowledge, you will lack power.

7 REASONS WHY YOU NEED TO PAY THE PRICE TO BE GREAT

(1) To serve God with peace of mind.

Lack of money is the root of all bitterness. Prosperity makes life enjoyable; life becomes boring when there is no money because of money answereth all things, according to

Ecclesiastes 10:19. A man without money will not have a settled mind, his mind will be trouble. Anointing without money can cause annoyance.

(2) To finance the work of God.
The work of God needs money to move forward, if you don't pay the price, you can't become great to partake in the great commission (Evangelism). For the gospel to reach another part of the world, money is required. Many dreams die as a result of lack of money to execute them, a lot of people have a big project and there is no money to run the project. You must pay the price of prayer if you desire to result in life.

(3) To take care of your family
The Bible makes it clear that anyone who cannot provide for his own, especially for that of his own house is worse than an unbeliever, 1Timothy 5:8. You need to pay the price of greatness to meet the requirements of raising and maintaining responsible children. If you as a father, you can't cater for your children, they may end up being armed robbers or prostitutes.

(4) For people to see the evidence of your Christianity
If you call yourself a Christian and you are poor, unbelievers may find it difficult to accept your God. No result, no respect.

(5) To be a blessing to others
In Genesis 12:2 God said, "And I will make of thee a great nation, and I will bless thee, and make thy name great, and thou shalt be a blessing." This promise is for every bonafide

child of God. God blesses you so that you can be a blessing to others, not to live a flamboyant life.

(6) To leave inheritance for your Children
Proverbs 13:22 says, "A good man leaveth an inheritance to his children." Imagine a man that died to leave nothing behind. The financial security of your family must be of concern to you. You must plan to leave something tangible for your children before you die, don't die empty or leave debt behind.

(7) To plan for your Retirement
Many people on earth don't plan to retire; they want to work until they die. There is time for everything, time to work and time to retire from work. To depend on your children financially when you are old is wrong, if you plan well, all will be well when you are old.

PRAYER BOMB

(1) Father, I thank you for giving me the grace to pay the price of greatness, in Jesus name.
(2) Thou power of greatness from heaven, overshadow me, in Jesus name.
(3) Father, let every dormant potential inside of me, receive fire and become active, in Jesus name.
(4) My Father my Father, every great price that I need to pay to become great in life, I receive grace to pay it, in Jesus name.

(5) Father, let every spirit of setback causing backwardness in my life; leave my life now by fire, in Jesus name.

(6) Father, I erase every mark of the tail from my life, in Jesus name.

(7) Father, let every power of little affecting my greatness in life, become powerless by fire, in Jesus name.

(8) Father, I receive power to pay the price that can provoke heaven to open for me, in Jesus name.

(9) Father, catapult me to the top of prosperity, in Jesus name.

(10) I decree in the name of Jesus, money, you will never be a problem to me as long as I live, in Jesus name.

(11) Father, I receive the spirit of excellent to excel in life, in Jesus name.

(12) Father, let every spirit of backwardness resisting me from moving forward in life, receive fire and leave my life, in Jesus name.

(13) Thou power that fell down the wall of Jericho, fall upon every problem in my life, in Jesus name.

(14) Father, if they have not been making it in my family, I will make it, in Jesus name.

(15) My destiny receives good things of life and rejects bad things of life, in Jesus name.

(16) My glory and star, arise by fire and shine worldwide, in Jesus name.

(17) Father, let my covenant right of prosperity locate me and manifest by fire, in Jesus name.

(18) Father, let every generational curse of rising and fall affecting my destiny, break by fire, in the name of Jesus.

(19) Father, every spirit of death from the pit of hell saying it is my turn to die, you are a liar, receive fire and perish, in Jesus name.

(20) Father, in my generation, please make me among the great and influential people, in Jesus name.

DAY TWENTY-FIVE

OPEN YOUR DOOR WITH THE KEY OF PRAYER

Text: James 5:16-18

Thunder Quote: (A closed mouth is a destiny closed.)

Every door has a key designed for it from the manufacturer to open it, but there is a special key called the master key that can open any door. There is a God that can open any door without using key, in Acts 12:5-10, Peter was kept in the prison, bind with chains and was sleeping in between two soldiers, when the one that open doors without using key came, he entered the prison, woke Peter up and led him out of the prison. The Bible says in verse six of Act 10, "When they were past the first and second ward, they came unto the iron gate that leadeth unto the city, which opened to them of his own accord." That door that leads to your promise-land that the enemy had shut is opened now, in Jesus name.

There is a God that has the key of David, that open and no man can shut, and shut which no man can open, he said in Revelation 3:8b, "behold I have set before thee an open door, and no man can shut it." That door that God himself has opened in your life, will remain open, in Jesus name. If you refuse to apply the key of prayer to your door, you will be locked outside and you will experience a permanently closed door in life. A closed mouth is a destiny closed. Many destinies are shut because many people refuse to open their mouth and pray violently. In verse sixteen of our Bible text, it says,

"The effectual fervent prayer of a righteous man availeth much." When you pray fervently and violently, your prayer will produce result instantly. For your door to be opened, you must be ready without ceasing. The day you stop praying you have given the enemy the invitation to attack. A prayerful man is a powerful man and a prayer less man is a powerless man. For you to access your door of a miracle, you must pray violently, because to break through, you must pray violently.

In Corinthians 16:9, the Bible says "for a great door and effectual is opened unto me, and there are many adversaries" For every great door, there is a great enemy, for every next level, there is a devil you must defeat. I command in the name of Jesus, every enemy between you and your open door shall die by fire, in Jesus name. And every enemy waiting for you as you move from one level to the other will perish by fire. After the children of Israel succeeded in leaving Egypt after many years of bondage and hard labor, the Red sea stood as an obstacle against them to enter their promised land. Eventually, God made a way of escape for them, they crossed the Red Sea, besides, and the land of Canaan is their target. For them to possess the land Canaan, there were giants they must defeat. Every enemy you refuse to kill will definitely kill you. In the University of Victory, you must win the battle if you want to be a champion. The enemy you fail to kill now will come after you later.

I have said it often, the only language the devil understands is violent, and you must be violent in prayer if you desire an open door in life. In James 5:17-18, Elijah prayed earnestly and rain refused to fall for three and a half year, and he prayed he prayed again, and rain fell. When you become an addicted prayer person, you will enjoy open doors in life. Many Christians are weak spiritually because they are lazy in the place of prayer. A book says, One week without prayers makes a man weak. If your prayer life is not charged with prayers, there is no way you can ever be in charge. In Act 16, Paul and Silas were put in the prison, they decided to pray and sing praises unto God, and God came in form of an earthquake and shake the foundation of the prison and all the doors of the prison were opened. I command every good door shut against you to open and remain open, in Jesus name. Psalm 24:7 says, "Lift up your heads, o ye gates; and be lifted up ye everlasting doors, and the king of glory shall come in." By the mandate of the Trinity, every good gate and everlasting door shall open for you today, in Jesus name.

Initially, I said that there is a God that can open and no man can shut, and shut and no man can open. If that same God says in His word in Revelation 3:8a, that he has set before you an open door that no man can shut, it means no man, demon, principalities, and powers can ever shut the door God has opened for you.

PRAYER BOMB

1. Father, I thank you for giving me the key of David, to open every closed door in my life, in Jesus name.
2. Father, let every door of blessing, that sees me and close, open now by fire, in Jesus name.

3. Father, let every demon assigned to monitor my door of breakthrough, success, promotion, and testimony receives fire and die by fire, in Jesus name.
4. Father, let every good door shut against me, open and remain permanently open, in Jesus name.
5. Father, I receive the power to pray violently and get out of every satanic problem, in Jesus name.
6. Father, every evil gate erected against me, I uproot and destroy it, in Jesus name.
7. God of Elijah, come down by the fire, and roast by fire anyone and everyone closing my door of blessing, in Jesus name.
8. My Father my Father, let every giant occupying my promise land, fall down and die, in Jesus name.
9. Father, open door of riches and wealth, in my life that nobody can ever shut, in Jesus name.
10. Father, secure my door of a miracle for me against every spiritual thief, in Jesus name.
11. Father, let every door of limitation constructed to hinder me from getting to my land of a miracle, scatter by fire.
12. Father, let every satanic gateman organized from the pit of hell, to close any good door open in my life, receive Holy Ghost fire, in Jesus name.
13. Holy Ghost fire, enter my life and turn me into a fire brand vessel, in Jesus name.
14. Father, I receive the key of David and I unlock every door closed against my business, in Jesus name.
15. Father, let every satanic padlock the enemy has used to lock my door of financial breakthrough, cut into a piece, in Jesus name.

16. Father, shut the evil doors in my life, and open the good doors in my life, in Jesus name.
17. Father, every back door opened by the enemy to take good things away from me, I close it permanently, in Jesus name.
18. Father, I recover back every missing key that I need to access my door of greatness, in Jesus name.
19. Father, let every door that I knock on from today, open by fire, in Jesus name.
20. My door of breakthrough, miracle, blessing, and testimony, open now and remain permanently open, in Jesus name.

DAY TWENTY-SIX

BREAKING RECORDS WITH YOUR GIFT TO PROVOKE HEAVEN

Text: 1 Kings 3:1-5, 9-14, 1 Kings 9:1-3

Thunder Quote: (When you give God the best, you will get the best from God.)

Life is full of so many secrets. The secret of life is in the hand of the Almighty God. For you to get secret about anything in life, you need to know God. The word of God says the secret things belong to God, but he has revealed it to his children-Deuteronomy 29:29. In Amos 3:7, the Bible says, "Surely the Lord GOD will do nothing, but he revealeth his secret unto his servants the Prophets." Information is power when you are not informed, you will be deformed. When God reveals the secret of your enemy to you, your enemy is in trouble.

Also, when you discover the secret of life, your life will be heaven on earth. Only a few people have discovered the secret of life, no wonder, only a few are on the top while many are on the ground floor. That was why I said that the secret things are in God's hand, and for God to reveal things to you, you must have a good relationship with him. The Bible says, "Solomon loved the LORD, walking in the statutes of David his father, 1Kings 3:3a. Remember, David, the father of Solomon was a man after God's heart; I guess his father would have told him the secret of how to become a man after God's heart. Let's consider some secrets about life.

(i)   The secret of Prosperity is in God's hand: 111 John 2.

(ii) The secret of Promotion is in God's hand: Psalm 75:6-7.

(iii) The secret of Victory is in God's hand: Exodus 14:14.

(iv) The secret of Fruitfulness is in God's hand: Genesis 1:28.

(v)   The secret of Protection is in God's hand: Psalm 91:1.

The reason why many people are still in one spot, sharing the same testimony or repeating the previous year in another year, is because they are still applying the same formula, they lack secrets of new things. If you keep applying the same formula to anything, you will always arrive at the same answer.

If you want a change in your life, you must change the way you have been doing things. God won't change your level if you are not determining to change. Solomon changed his mentality toward giving and obtained a blank cheque of a miracle. The secret of living is giving. If you want to live in prosperity, you must give violently. In Proverbs 18:16, the Bible says, "A man's gift maketh room for him, and bringeth him before the great man." The gift we are talking about is not your potential, talent or academic qualification; it is your material possession or money.

Sacrificing things that will cost you something, things you cherish most, valuable and precious things. For instance, when you empty your account for the gospel, giving your best car for evangelism or giving God 90% of your tithe. Breaking record means when someone beat the best performance or most remarkable event of its kind that has been officially recognized. Solomon was a record breaker as long as giving is concerned, he gave an offering that nobody has ever given and heaven opened. I pray for you by the power in the name of Jesus, God will turn you into a record breaker.

Who is a record breaker? A record breaker is a person that achieves a better result or higher level that has never been achieved before. In Luke 5:1-7, Peter broke the record as long as fishing is concerned, to the extent that he mobilizes his colleagues to help him. The Bible says, in verse six of Luke chapter five "they enclosed a great multitude of fishes: and their net brake." Some record breakers are; the richest men and most brilliant students etc. Solomon broke the record in his generation. I decree upon you, in your generation, you will be among the people that matter! When they are mentioning the names of those that affect their generation, they will mention your name, in the name of Jesus. Jabez was a nonentity that provoked heaven, and today his name is mentioned in the Bible. People may not know you now, but before you leave this universe, God will turn you into an icon of prosperity, a needed man and a demand globally.

You can't give what you don't have. When you give God the best, you will get the best from God. What and how you give to God will determines how you love God. An ingrate, stingy or greedy person will always find it difficult to give to God even when the Holy Spirit is ministering to him, that money has become a god in your hands. If you truly love God, you can give him all, even empty all your bank account for him. Giving is from the heart, if you don't have a giving heart or a giving spirit, giving is excluded from the dictionary of your destiny. You can't help God to be wealthy, he is a wealthy God, your money or gift can't make God rich. Don't ever think that you are helping God when you give; you are only helping yourself to be great. When you empty your account for God, a permanent open heaven will be open for you. It is more blessed to give than to receive, givers never lack. The quality of the gift you present to God will determine the quantity of God's blessing upon you. Do you know that God knows your worth? You must understand this secret, anytime you give God, you are lending to God, Proverb 19:17. God blessed you so that you can be a blessing to others.

PRAYER BOMB

1. Father, I thank you for the grace to break the record with the gifts you have given to me, in Jesus name.
2. Father, turn me into a record breaker in my generation, in Jesus name.
3. Father, change every spirit of love of money in my life, to love of Christ, in Jesus name.
4. My Father my Father, turn me into a violent giver in your Church, to humanity, and in my generation, in Jesus name.
5. Father, reveal the secret of true prosperity to me so that I can become a prosperous person, in Jesus name.
6. Father, give me a giving heart and a giving spirit to be a giver, in Jesus name.
7. Father, overshadow my destiny with your oil of gladness above my entire mates, in Jesus name.

8. Father, baptize me with an excellent spirit that will make me a needed man in my generation, in Jesus name.
9. Father, let every spirit of ingrate, stinginess, greediness operating in my life, come out by fire, in Jesus name.
10. Father, let the greatness inside me, receive the fire of the Holy Ghost and begin to manifest, in Jesus name.
11. Father, every record I need to break to move to the next level, I break it, in Jesus name.
12. Father, let my gifts in form of money, material things, I have given in the house of God, make way for me now, in Jesus name.
13. Father, I receive power to pay the price of greatness to become a great man, in Jesus name.
14. Father, by the power in the name of Jesus, let heaven of miracles, signs, and wonders, open permanently in my life, in Jesus name.
15. Father, because you are the all sufficient God, turn all my demand to supply, in Jesus name.
16. Father, include my name among men that matters in my generation, in Jesus name.
17. My Father my Father, let your divine favor come upon me, and bring a total transformation into my life, in Jesus name.
18. Father, let every power of darkness closing the heaven over my life, receive fire and scatter by fire, in Jesus name.
19. Father, give me divine wisdom that exceeds the wisdom of men, in Jesus name.
20. Father, give me the secret of life so that my life will be heaven on earth, in Jesus name.

DAY TWENTY-SEVEN

ENLARGE MY COAST

Text: Genesis 12:1-4 and Genesis 13:14-17

Thunder Quote: (How large your coast is, will determine the size of your dream.)

Lot became an obstacle in the life of Abraham the day he started following him. Until you separate yourself from that Lot, you won't experience enlargement in your life. The Lot could be unfriendly friends, household enemy, relatives, boss, neighbor, business partner, principalities, and powers. You are mandated to be fruitful and multiply. In Joshua 1:3-4, the Bible says, "Every place that the sole of your feet shall tread upon, that I have given unto you, as I said unto Moses. From the wilderness and this Lebanon even unto the great river, the river Euphrates, all the land of the Hittites, and unto the great sea toward the going down of the sun, shall be your coast."

Some people need to be separated from you so that the original plan of God can come to manifestation in your life. The day Lot separated himself from Abraham in Genesis 13:14-16, God told him to lift up his eyes and look the northward, southward, eastward and westward that all the land that he can see belong to him, God also told him to walk through the length and breadth, that they are all his. Who is the Lot in your life? The fire of the Holy Ghost will separate him from you, in Jesus name.

Enlarge means, to make something bigger, to extend, to expand or increase in capacity or scope. In Judges 6:14-16, when God told Gideon that he is going to save Israel from the hands of the Midianites, Gideon replied in verse fourteen, "my family is poor in Manasseh, and I am the least in my father's house." God is not a respecter of person; he can use anybody to fulfill his purpose. Your size, age, color, tribe or family is not a barrier when God has decided to use you. I pray for a reader of this book, people may not know you now, but I decree in the name of Jesus before you die, the world will hear about you, when they are mentioning the names of people that affected their generation, you will be among them; in Jesus name.

If you don't make history in this world before you die, coming to the world will look as if you have only taken a stroll. In Chronicles 4:9-10, Jabez refused to allow his family background to put him on the ground so that he won't end up a nonentity, he cried to his God violently because he was tired of his condition, the Bible says in verse ten, "And Jabez called on God of Israel, saying oh that thou wouldest bless me indeed and enlarge my coast, and that thine hand might be with me, and that thou wouldest keep me from evil, that it may not grieve me, And God granted him that which he request."

The day you get dissatisfied with your condition, victory is certain. Many people are not tired of their problem, some are so complacent in life, and they remain the same. There was a guy I grew up with in Festac Town, Lagos State, Nigeria, whenever I come around, I discovered he still lives in his father's house at 42 years old, not working and he is not married. A lot of people are wasting time on earth; I pray for you, you will not die until you fulfill your destiny, in Jesus name. When you are wasting time, you are wasting life. Jabez called on God to enlarge his coast because he discovered that his coat was too small.

How large your coast is, will determine the size of your dream, limiting who you can be, is limiting who you will be. There is no limit for enlargement of your coast, except the once you create for yourself. As a man thinketh in his heart, so he is. Your mind is a drawing board that you can write your vision on. Make up your mind to get dissatisfied with the size of vision. Your limitation is not a function of your condition; it is a function of your decision. When you make up your mind, to get what you want with a deadline, God will teach you how to get it. Jabez made up his mind. Nothing moves until you move, the world only moves for a man who moves, when you make a move, things will begin to move.

Many people are comfortable with their present level, which is the reason why they don't attain the next level. Success will not come to you where you are; you have to go where it is.

7 PEOPLE THAT EXPERIENCED ENLARGEMENT OF COAST

(1) Abraham, Gen. 13:2, 6 from ordinary man to a great man.

(2) Solomon, 1 Kings 4:29-30, 1Kings 3:12-13, from wise man to the wisest man.

(3) Obed-edom, 11 Sam 6:11, from gate-man to great-man.

(4) Joseph, Gen 37-Gen 41, from Slave to Prime Minister.

(5) David, 1 Samuel 16:11-13 from Shepherd to a King.

(6) Jabez, 1 Chronicles 4:9-10 from nobody to somebody.

(7) The widow in 11 Kings 4:1-7, from Debtor to Creditor.

9 APPARATUS THAT CAN ENLARGE YOUR COAST

(1) God   John 15:5c

(2) Obedience   Isaiah 1:19

(3) Humility   James 4:10

(4) Determination   Daniel 1:8

(5) Diligence   Proverb 22:29

(6) Prayer   Mark 11:24

(7) Fasting   Isaiah 40:31

(8) Faith   Hebrews 10:38a

(9) Giving   Luke 6:38

PRAYER BOMB

(1) Father, I thank you because you have enlarged my coast, in Jesus name.

(2) Father, let every Lot partnering with me, be separated by fire, in Jesus name.

(3) Father, enlarge the coast of my destiny, in Jesus name.

(4) Father, don't let me waste time in this world becoming nobody, in Jesus name.

(5) Father, visit the foundation of my destiny with your power, in Jesus name.

(6) My Father my Father, I command every spirit of complacent in my life, to leave by fire, in Jesus name.

(7) Father, let anyone or anybody using evil power to monitor the affairs of my life die by fire, in Jesus name.

(8) Father, let every principality and power attacking the progress of my life, receive fire and scatter by fire, in Jesus name.

(9) Father, let every satanic assembly gathering against my destiny, scatter by fire, in Jesus name.

(10) Father, wherever the enemy has tied my glory from shining, I untie it by fire, in Jesus name.

(11) Father, give me the power to affect my generation and make history before I die, in Jesus name.

(12) Father, let every life style of mediocrity affecting your original plans for my life, receive fire and be destroyed, in Jesus name.

(13) My Father my Father, let every power that has determined to terminate me, be terminated by fire, in Jesus name.

(14) Father, let every satanic boundary or limitation mounted against my destination, scatter by fire, in Jesus name.

(15) Father, let every great dream and vision in me, manifest by fire, in Jesus name.

(16) Father, wherever my person cannot take to, let your grace take me there, in Jesus name.

(17) Father, I revoke every evil decree upon my life with the blood of Jesus.

(18) Father, endorse my name in the register of testified, in Jesus name.

(19) Father, let every darkness surrounding my destiny, receive light from heaven and vanish, in Jesus name.

(20) Father, I cancel by fire every satanic strategy on assignment to alter my vision, in Jesus name.

DAY TWENTY-EIGHT

IT IS MY SET TIME OF SETTLEMENT

TEXT: Genesis 18:1-14, Genesis 21:2

Thunder Quote: (Giving God a set time doesn't change his own time.)

God can decide to delay is time, but he cannot deny his word. Delay is not denial, God works with time. You can't decide the time for God, he decided on his own. No matter the time you set to achieve anything in life, it doesn't change God's time. Even if God does not do it, it does not change the fact that he is God. Note, that God is not a late comer; he comes, at his own time. If you are expecting God to come now, he can decide to come in 10 years time. God has a specific time for everyone. In Ecclesiastes 3:1, to everything there is a season and a time to every purpose under the heaven. God has a time-table for all his children. The fact that you belong to God, you are on his timetable of blessing, promotion, favor, miracle, and testimony.

God's time is different from man's time, nobody can stop him, or question him because He is the best time keeper and time manager. Heaven will declare today as your day of settlement, in Jesus name. The time you have been waiting for has come, embrace your miracle now by faith. Before time came into existence, God has been existing, that is the reason why he has the power to create and control time. Genesis 8:22, says, "While the earth remaineth, seed time and harvest and cold and heat and summer and winter, and day and night shall not cease." The one that created a thing has control over the thing. Giving God a set time doesn't change His own time, there is time for everything. Ecclesiastes 9:11 says, "I returned and saw under the sun, that the race is not to the swift, nor the battle to the strong, neither yet bread to the wise, nor yet riches to men of understanding nor yet favor to men of skill; but time and chance happeneth to them all." When God decided to attend to you according to His time, there is nobody that can stop Him. This season, The Almighty God will attend to you, in Jesus name. When God says it is time, it is time, your doubt or unbelief can't alter His plan. In Genesis 18:10-14, when God told Abraham that his wife Sarah is going to have a child, Sarah laughed because she knows within herself that she has passed the period of menopause, she was very old, and she can't have pleasure in sex, God responded, is anything too hard for the Lord? If the one that created time says, by this time tomorrow your level will change; your doubt can't change His word. The word of God says, God honors His word, and in Psalm 119:89, "Forever, O LORD, thy word is settled in heaven." I decree into your life, every word concerning you, is settled in Heaven, receive divine settlement in every aspect of your life, in Jesus name.

Menopause is not meno-stop, most of the fantastic testimonies shared in the Church always passed through the process of delay before manifesting. Before settlement, a price most have been paid. In Genesis 29:18-21, after Jacob served Laban for seven years for his daughter Rachel, he demanded his right, in verse 21, the Bible says, "And Jacob said unto Laban, ''Give me my wife, for my days, are fulfilled that I may go in unto her." Your labor will not be in vain, in Jesus name. I don't know that person you have worked for and have refused to pay you; they will not have rest of mind until you are paid, in Jesus name. 1Peter 5:10 says, "But the God of all grace, who hath called us unto his eternal glory by Christ Jesus, after that ye have suffered a while, make you perfect, stablish, strengthen, settle you." Please note, you are not going to suffer forever, it is for a while. I pray for you, with effect from today, all your suffering since you came into this world shall turn to enjoyment, in Jesus name.

10 THINGS YOU NEED TO DO WHEN YOU'VE NOT BEEN SETTLED

1. Examine yourself and ask yourself the following question; am I doing the right business? Do I pay my tithe? Is God pleased with me? Is there any seed of pride or forgiveness in me? Did I have God's approval? Am I married according to the will of God? Am I the enemy of myself?
2. Develop a rugged faith.
3. Be patience. Hebrew 11:36, ye have need of patience; that after ye have done the will of God, ye might receive the promise.
4. Embark on fasting.
5. Hold God to his word.
6. Change your gear to praise. God inhabits praise, Psalm 22:3. Praise moves God to do the impossible.
7. Pray until something happens, PUSH. 1Thes 5:17, pray without ceasing.

8. Make a vow to God. When Hannah decided to make a vow to God in 1 Sam 1:11, her prayer request was sealed and she became a mother.
9. Ask God for mercy. In Rom 9:15 says "God will have mercy on whom he will have mercy." Also in Luke 23:42-43, one of the thieves that were crucified with Jesus was forgiven and ends up in paradise with "Jesus because of mercy.
10. Be thankful. In 1Thessalonians 5:18, in everything give thanks, for this is the will of God in Christ concerning you. Thanksgiving compelled God to do more than what is expected. When you learn how to thank God, your tank of blessing will be full.

PRAYER BOMB

1. Father, I thank you because it is time to settle me, in Jesus name.
2. Father, I have suffered enough, please arise in your mercy and settle me, in Jesus name.
3. Father, my time of settlement is now; please settle me, in Jesus name.
4. Father, let every power of darkness shifting the date of my testimony; receive the fire of the Holy Ghost and scatter, in Jesus name.
5. Father, let every spirit of delay, delaying my time of miracle; catch fire, in Jesus name.
6. My Father my Father, let every time waster, leave my life now, in Jesus name.

7. God of restoration, restore back all my wasted years of opportunity to become great, in Jesus name.
8. My glory, my star, and destiny come out of obscurity and begin to shine, in Jesus name.
9. Father, I decree in the name of Jesus, let there be light in life, business, marriage, and finance, in Jesus name.
10. Father, let every destiny killer, star hunter, and dream killer after my life; perish by fire, in Jesus name.
11. My Father my Father, let every prince in the region of my location assigned to hinder my prayer, receive the fire of the Holy Ghost and perish, in Jesus name.
12. Father, put my name on the time table of favor, in Jesus name.
13. My destiny helpers, wherever you are, located me now, in Jesus name.
14. Father, please suspend everything you are doing and attend to me now, in Jesus name.
15. My set time of favor, promotion, elevation, next level and financial break through, manifest by fire, in Jesus name.
16. My Father, my Father, please in your mercy, declare today as my day of divine settlement, in Jesus name.
17. Father, I receive divine speed to overtake all my mates that have gone ahead of me in life, in Jesus name.
18. God the Father, God the Son and God the Holy Spirit, intervene and change my story today, in Jesus name.
19. My Father my Father, I am getting old every day, please remember before it is too late, in Jesus name.
20. Father, all my entitlements in the hand of anybody, I receive it back by fire by force, in Jesus name.

DAY TWENTY-NINE
WORK HARD BEFORE IT GETS HARD
Text: Ecclesiastes 9:10-12

Thunder Quote: (You either work hard now and enjoy later or enjoy now and suffer later.)

Hard work is part of life. If you don't work hard now, it will be hard in the future. When you have a handwork, life won't be hard for you. In our text, the Bible says, "Whatsoever thy hand findeth to do." God did not specify the kind of work. It could be; selling palm oil, Tailoring, Teaching Driver etc. God wants you to be busy doing something instead of being idle. Many people pray amiss or ignorantly that God should bless the work of their hand when they don't have any handwork at hand. It is better to say, God gives me work.

John 5:17, "Jesus said, my father worketh hitherto and I work." If the God that created all things worked and is still working, then you must work. In John 9:4, Jesus said again, I must work the works of Him that sent me, while it is the day, the night cometh when no man can work. You still have time now to go to school, acquire Skills or, learn hand-work before you get old. Time wait for nobody, there is time for everything. There is time to work and there is time to rest. Don't use your time of retirement to work.

You either work hard now and enjoy later or enjoy now and suffer later. If you want to eat big in future, work hard now. Many old gatemen would have been great, but they refused to work while their mates were working; today, they are opening the gate for their children's mates. God hates an idle or lazy man, he can't bless a lazy man. All those that become great in the Bible and in history worked hard. If you don't work hard now you will end up being a burden or a liability to your spouse, family, neighbor, nation and even the Church.

I once told a friend that, if you can't feed yourself well with the work you are doing now, please don't go into marriage, if you don't want to endure and manage life, because your wife may end up leaving you. Feed yourself well before you feed others. You can't give what you don't have. It is better you look for a job that can sustain you and your family. Life is expensive and taking care of family is also expensive. 1Timothy 5:8 says, "If a man does not provide for his family and especially for his immediate family, he has denied the faith and is worst than an infidel." It is how you lay your bed that you will lay on it, what you give to life will determine what you will get from it. If you refuse to work hard, you will suffer. Lack of proper planning will make a man end up begging his mates to survive. 11Thessalonians 3:10, "No food for a lazy man." I read a book that says, Poverty is the certificate given to a lazy man.

According to Genesis Chapter two, after God created Adam, the first assignment God gave Adam was to dress the garden of Eden.

You need to work hard for posterity sake. Proverbs 13:22, "A good man leaveth an inheritance to his children's children." If you don't pay the price of greatness, you will never become great in life, and greatness will only end in your lips. The way you handle your life now will determine whether life will be easy or hard for you in the future.

10 KEY THAT STAIR UP HARD WORK

1. Perseverance
2. Wisdom- proverb 4:7.
3. Diligent- Proverb 29:18.
4. Vision- proverb 29 29:18.
5. Determination. Daniel 1:8.
6. Obedience- Isaiah 1:19.
7. Humility- James 4:10.
8. Faith – Hebrew 4:10.
9. Fasting and prayer.
10. God -Luke 1:37.

PRAYER BOMB

1. My hands, my hands, in the name of Jesus, receive power to work and make money, in Jesus name.
2. Father, deliver me from every spirit of joblessness and idleness, in Jesus name.
3. Spirit of Laziness and thoughtfulness, leave my life now, in Jesus name.
4. Father, I wash my hands with the blood of Jesus against the profitless effort, in Jesus name.
5. Father, bless the work of my hands with the result, in Jesus name.
6. Every spirit of regret awaiting me in future, I come against you now, in Jesus name
7. Father, I receive power from heaven to pay the price of greatness and to become great, in Jesus name.
8. Father, let every principality and power against my destiny; catch fire now, in Jesus name.
9. Any strong man or strong woman monitoring my progress, receive fire and die by fire, in Jesus name.
10. Father, give me an idea to become great among my mates in my generation, in Jesus name.
11. Father, every mark of tail placed upon me, I wash it off, in Jesus name.
12. Father, every spirit of working hard without any visible result, leave my life, in Jesus name.
13. Father, give me the formula of divine prosperity, in Jesus name.
14. My Father my Father, turn all my years of hard labor to favor today, in Jesus name.

15. Father, let every spirit of almost there affecting my destiny, be destroyed by the fire of the Holy Ghost, in Jesus name.
16. Father, bless the work of my hands so that begging and borrowing will end in my life, in Jesus name.
17. Father, let every garment of financial bondage the enemy had forced on me; catch fire, in Jesus name.
18. Father, let every spirit of working like an Elephant and reaping like an ant, in my life, get out by fire, in Jesus name.
19. Father, with effect from today, I will work little and earn a plenty profit, in Jesus name.
20. Father, let divine favor, that turn labor to favor come upon me, in Jesus name.

DAY THIRTY

PURSUE, OVERTAKE AND RECOVER All

Text: 1Samuel 30:1-8, 18-19.

Thunder Quote: (You can't win any battle without the help of God.)

The day you stop weeping over a particular problem and do something about it, that marks the end of the problem because you have taken a step. There is no problem that you weep, complain or murmur over that leaves, weeping never solve a problem, it only fuels it, and that is, it increases the problem. The moment you become determined and encourage yourself over issues of life, the end has come over that issue. Every problem that has a manufacturing date also has an expiring date. I decree, by the power in the name of Jesus, before sunrise tomorrow, that stubborn problem in your life will expire, in the name of Jesus.

The day you become paranoid over a particular issue, victory is certain. In our text, David and his men wept over the Calamity that happened to them when their enemies came and invaded their camp, the Bible says, they weep until they had no power to weep again but the situation was still the same.

Until David encourage himself in the Lord, the situation was still the same. From today, everything causing you to weep will turn to a laughing testimony, in Jesus name; you will always have a reason to laugh every moment for your life, in Jesus mighty name. David invited God by making an inquiry. The reason why many people stay too long in their problem is that they failed to bring God in; they prefer to handle the matter by themselves. You can't win any battle without the help of God. The Bible says, the battle is not yours; it is the LORD's battle. In Exodus 14, when the children of Israel left Egypt, they came in contact with the Red Sea and their leader Moses, told them in verse fourteen, "The LORD shall fight for you, and ye shall hold your peace." If the children of Israel had decided to fight the enemy by themselves, it is either they perish or go back to Egypt. I pray for you with effect from today, God will not stop fighting for you, in Jesus name! The mighty man in battle will always rescue you in the time of battle, in Jesus name! You will always win in every battle because you are more than a conqueror, in the name of Jesus.

Don't embark on any battle without the approval of God. In 1Samuel 30:8 the Bible says, And David inquired of the LORD, saying, Shall I pursue after this troop? Shall I overtake them? And He answered him, Pursue; for thou shalt surely overtake them, and without fail to recover all."

Listen, when God decided to back you up, be rest assures he will, when God promises, he never fails. He didn't say David will recover some, he said all, which is the reason why I have good news for someone reading this book; you will recover all that the enemy has taken from you before finish reading this book, in Jesus name. For you to recover all, you must surrender all to the Almighty. In Matthew 6:33, the Bible says, "seek, ye first the kingdom of God and his righteousness and all these things shall be added unto you." In 1Samuel 28:6 says, "And when Saul inquired of the LORD, the LORD answered him, neither by dreams, nor by Urim, nor by Prophets." Due to the disobedient of Saul, God stop speaking to him, and he had to began to seek other means of power, and in Chapter thirty-one of first Samuel, he died mysteriously, he was beheaded and his three Sons died the same day with him. You can only recover all, if God is with you, if not your case will be like the one of Saul. I pray that every disobedience that will end your life early, you won't go into it, in Jesus name.

7 THINGS THAT HELPED DAVID TO RECOVER ALL

(1) THE presence of God: The presence of God gives Victory. Anywhere you go without God may land you in trouble. When God goes ahead of you in any battle, you are safe. Isaiah 45:2
(2) Endurance: David endure despite all that happened to him before he recovered, he didn't give up. If you can endure, you will enjoy at the end.
(3) Courage: A discourage man can never win in life, a discouraged man is frustrated, person. Destiny will be aborted where there is no courage.
(4) Determination: There is no limitation on what you want to be if you can give it what it takes (Bishop Benson Idahosa). Nothing is impossible to a willing heart.
(5) He forgot the Past: Yesterday's failures are today's seeds. The fact that you failed yesterday does not mean you will fail today. God never consults your past to determine your future (Mike Murdock). When you are down on your back, if you can look up, you can get up (Les Brown).

(6) Perseverance: By perseverance, the snail reached the ark (Charles H. Spurgeon). Those who persevere are the one left standing when everyone else quits.

(7) Joy: David changed his gear from weeping to joy. Joy gives strength because the Joy of the Lord is our strength. Weeping may endure for a night but joy cometh in the morning-Psalm 30:5.

PRAYER BOMB

(1) Father, I thank you because today, I shall recover all my blessings from the hands of my enemies, in Jesus name.

(2) Father, I receive power from above to pursue, overtake and recover back all my lost and stolen blessing from the enemies, in Jesus name.

(3) My Father my maker, I decree in the name of Jesus, no more loss of my life, business, marriage, and family, in Jesus name.

(4) Father, let every spirit of discouragement occupying my life, get out by fire, in Jesus name.

(5) Father, let every satanic thief assigned to steal anything that belongs to me, die by fire, in Jesus name.

(6) Father, don't let me weep over any members of my family and don't let anyone weep over me, in Jesus name.

(7) Father, I command every problem bringing shame and disgrace to my life, to expire now, in the name of Jesus.

(8) Father, let every storm from the pit of hell troubling my life, my business and family, cease by fire, in Jesus name.

(9) Any satanic visitor living in my life, pack your load and go, in Jesus name.

(10) God of Abraham, Isaac, and Jacob, let your presence go ahead of me wherever I go from today, in Jesus name.

(11) The fire of the Holy Ghost; locate every enemy planning to attack me by fire, in Jesus name.

(12) Father, I hand over to you every battle waiting for me in the future, fight for me, in Jesus name.

(13) Father, from now hence forth, my enemies will not rejoice over me again, in Jesus name.

(14) Father, let every long time war, I have been fighting ever since I was born, come to an end now, in Jesus name.

(15) My Father my Father, come down by fire and consume every stubborn enemy desperate to truncate my destiny, in Jesus name.

(16) Father, please direct my destiny to the right direction, so that I won't be a mockery to my enemy, in Jesus name.

(17) Father, let every spirit of retrogression affecting my progress in life, come out by the fire and leave, in Jesus name.

(18) The God that answereth by fire, answer anyone and everyone asking me, where is my God by fire, in Jesus name.

(19) Father Lord, don't let me take any foolish decision that will land me in trouble, in Jesus name.

(20) Father, every road blocker on my road to breakthrough, clear and scatter by fire, in Jesus name.

DAY THIRTY-ONE

DON'T GIVE UP, HELP IS ON THE WAY

Text: 1 Kings 17:8-15

Thunder Quote: (Those who give up in life never go up in life.)

The widow in our Bible text, discouraged and tired of life due to austerity, she decided to commit suicide with her only son, thank God for sending his Prophet to rescue her and her son. Due to Poverty, their last meal was the only food left. God multiplied their last meal and they had abundant food in the house to eat.

Many people give up in life before the arrival of their miracle. It is unfortunate, that many are not aware that God is aware of their challenges. A young man graduated with 1st Class in the University, he decided to go to a particular city in search of Job, he submitted his CV in many organizations, expecting that he would be called for interviews. He waited one month, six months and a year, none of the organization called him, he was fed up and discouraged, packed his belongings and left the city back to his village. A day after he left, a post man brought a letter from an oil and gas firm, that he is urgently needed, 8 am the following day for an interview so that he can start working immediately. What a sad story, he had given up. Life is a School of no retreat, no surrender, in the University of Success, giving up is not allowed. Giving up is an attitude of a coward. Those who give up in life, never go up in life.

Champions never give up. You must have the mind of a winner if you want to be a winner. Life is an environment where only those that are determined stays. You must fight until you win, and keep winning until you become a winner. Most people on the top were once ex-losers who refuse to give up; there are vacancies at the top for the winner. Don't allow your background to put you on the ground. A lot of people give excuses in life for giving up. Bill gate was a drop out that went and reinforced and became a great man, Thomas Edison failed over 1000 times before discovering the ladder to success. No matter how many time you have failed, be determined and believe that you will bounce back again because a great future awaits you if you can hold to the end.

Tough time never last, but tough people do last - (Robert Schuller). Become tougher when the situation becomes though because the battle will become tough when you are about to win. Don't give up, I see help coming your way, don't give up. God is stepping in, don't give up, you are almost there. Winners don't quit and quitters don't win. Champion are not those who do not fail, but they are those who do not quit, no prize for quitters, victory will surely go to the one who never quit. Life is full of problems and obstacles; there is no man in this world without a problem.

Life is full of problems and obstacles; there is no man in this world without problem. Any man without a problem in this world is a problem to the world. Problems and obstacles can delay you temporarily, but you can stop yourself permanently. No condition is permanent, every end is a new beginning, and the end of one thing is the beginning of another thing. Don't give up; the last key may be the one that will open the door. Life is a challenge itself, and problems are constant in life. You must have this understanding, that you are not the first person to pass through what you are passing through. If you don't pass through, you won't breakthrough. You must also realize that your right living in God doesn't mean you won't encounter problems. Problems are the tonic of life that builds up our spiritual muscle to be fit to face life. If you don't pass anything made, you can't be anything-(Matthew Ashimolowo). Even the snail, the slowest animals refuse to give up until it enters Noah's ark.

You must not give up because God has not given up on your case. This year, by the power in the name of Jesus, God will settle you with an amazing miracle that will be beyond your human understanding. Those miracles you have been waiting for will arrive before you finish this 40 days and 40 nights spiritual exercise, in Jesus name. Before you even think of giving up, help will locate you, in Jesus name. Rise up, like a rugged soldier, and pray violently.

PRAYER BOMB

1. Father, I thank you for giving me the grace not to give up in life, in Jesus name.
2. Father, because you have not given up in my case, give me the grace never to give up in my case, give me the grace never to give up in life, in Jesus name.

3. My Father my Father, let every problem that is greater than me or beyond me, catch fire, in Jesus name.
4. Holy Ghost fire, destroy every power of delay, delaying the arrival of my miracle, in Jesus name.
5. Father, let every spirit of discouragement occupying my life, get out by fire, in Jesus name.
6. Father, I refuse to give up before the arrival of my promotion, breakthrough, and miracles this year, in Jesus name.
7. Oh Lord my God, please connect me back to my helpers before it is too late, in Jesus name.
8. Every evil voice from the graveyard or mortuary advising me to commit suicide. I silent you forever, in Jesus name.
9. Father, I receive the spirit of boldness and courage to withstand the test of life, in Jesus name.
10. My Father my maker, every spirit of late miracle following me, get out of my life now by fire, in Jesus name.
11. Father, please help me and send helpers to me by this time tomorrow, in Jesus name.
12. Father, my miracle, testimony, promotion letter, contract, and breakthrough, manifest by fire in Jesus name.
13. Heaven and earth, co-operate together now and release my entire withheld miracles today, in Jesus name.
14. Poverty, you are a stranger, get out of my life now by fire, in Jesus name.
15. My Father my maker, please deliver me from every life style of suffering, and struggling, in Jesus name.
16. Father, with effect from today, please change the standard of my living, in Jesus name.

17. Father, before the end of this 40 days and 40 nights spiritual exercise, give me an amazing miracle that will amaze all my enemies, in Jesus name.
18. Father, after this 40 days and 40 night exercise, make life easy for me and let me begin to enjoy the good things of Life, in Jesus name.
19. Oh Lord my God, let every force of darkness, forcing me to dwell in one position since the previous years, till now scatter by fire, in Jesus name.
20. Father, make my life meaningful, in Jesus name.

DAY THIRTY- TWO

AUTHORIZED TO BE FRUITFUL

Text: Genesis 1:27-28

Thunder Quote: (if you are faithful, you will be fruitful.)

Fruitfulness is your convenient right as a candidate of righteousness. The fact that you are a joint heir with Christ; you are mandated to be fruitful because it is already programmed into your destiny to be fruitful. I also want you to realize that it is on the platform of God's plan for you to be fruitful. In Jeremiah 29:11, God says, "For I know the thoughts that I think toward you, saith the Lord, thought of peace and not of evil, to give you an expected end." from our topic, we have two vital words authorized and fruitful.

Authorized from Oxford advanced learner's dictionary means, to give official permission for something or for somebody to do something. Permit me to say, by the permission of the Trinity, you are permitted to be, fruitful, in Jesus name. Fruitfulness, on the other hand, means, producing many useful results or abundant production. I degree into every ramification of life, from now hence forth, you shall be fruitful, in Jesus name. From the genesis of your life, it is already settled that you shall be fruitful, that is the reason why I have good news for you; by the statement issued to man by God according to Genesis 1:28, YOU SHALL BE FRUITFUL, IN JESUS NAME! Until you are fruitful you can never multiply. I declare into your life, in the name of Jesus, be fruitful and multiply in your

Marriage, business, and career, in Jesus name. Imagine a pawpaw tree without fruits; it can never multiply until it has fruits carrying seeds inside. In Ephesians 3:20, "Now unto him, that is able to do exceeding abundantly above all that we ask or think."

According to the definition of fruitfulness, I said, producing many useful results. Without the power of the Holy Ghost in a man, fruitfulness may be impossible. Without conceiving first, you can't have a child. You are programmed to produce many useful results in life. No result, no respect. You will be insulted if you have no result.

Have you been insulted, because of no result in your marriage or career, with effect from today, you shall be, a result producer, in Jesus name. Hannah was insulted by Penninah, in 1Samuel 1:6, because God shut her womb, and the Lord remembered Hannah and gave her children and the mouth of Penninah was shut permanently. I prophesy into your life today, that miracle that will silence anyone and everyone mocking you; receive it now, in Jesus name. I join my faith with your faith; you will never experience barrenness again, in Jesus name. This month, you shall be visited specially by God, I see God stepping into your problem and giving you a testimony that will turn you to a topic in your neighborhood, family, church, and place of work, in Jesus name.

Have you been barren for years; nine months from now, you will make the same statement Sarah made in Genesis 21:6, "And Sarah said, God had made me laugh so that all that hear will laugh with me." I see people gathering in your house for a naming ceremony. From today, God will put laughter in every word that proceeds out of your mouth, in Jesus name. Abraham's shut-cut, taking plan B due to delay in child bearing sleeping with Sarah maid was due to his unfaithful. Don't ever take shut cut in life because it can truncate one's destiny. Don't compromise your faith visiting a native doctor in search of children, money, wealth, promotion etc, please wait on God. In Job 14:14, Job says, "All the days of my appointed time, I will wait till my change come."Don't try to run faster than God, wait for your time, the delay is not denial, no condition is permanent, menopause is not menostop.

Weeping may endure for a night, but Joy comes in the morning. That shame and reproach that barrenness has brought into life, will vanish now, in Jesus name. Micah, one of David wives despised her husband, because her husband was praising God and she became barren for life, I pray for you seeking the face of God for fruitfulness, in any area of your life that there is a divine punishment upon you, due to what you have done in past, may God in His infinite mercy, be merciful to you and cause you to be fruitful, in Jesus name. Every divine punishment that has altered the original plan and purpose of God concerning you, may the blood of Jesus that was a shield on the cross of Calvary speak mercy for you, in the name of Jesus.

PRAYER BOMB

1. Father, I thank you because I'm mandated to be fruitful, in Jesus name.
2. Father, every covenant I have with the spirit of barrenness, I break it by fire, in name of Jesus
3. My Father my maker, according to your word in Gen 1:28, I shall be fruitful in every in every area of life, in Jesus name.
4. Father, I receive power to be fruitful and multiply in business, marriage, and career, in Jesus name.
5. Father, let every yoke of no result and lack of achievement placed upon me, received the fire of the Holy Ghost, in Jesus name.
6. Father, by the backing of Trinity, I contact power to become a result producer, in every ramification of life, in Jesus name.
7. Father, anyone and everyone laughing at me due to my present predicament. Lord, give me a breakthrough that will silence them, in Jesus name.
8. Father, step into every stubborn problem in my life that has turned me into an object of caricature before my fellow human-being, in Jesus name.
9. Father, every disgracing that have ridiculed me, take over and let it be over, in Jesus name.
10. Father, add laughter to every word that comes out of my mouth, in Jesus name
11. Father, enough is enough, put an end to barrenness in my life, in Jesus name.
12. My Father my creator, every short cut programmed by the devil to cut short my life, I reject it, in Jesus name.

13. Father, any divine punishment upon my life due to my past unfaithful, oh Lord, have mercy and deliver me, in Jesus name.
14. Every hereditary curse of barrenness upon my life, break, in Jesus name.
15. Father, every area of my life that barrenness has taken charge, reverse it to fruitfulness, in Jesus name.
16. Father, let every spirit and demon of barrenness leave my life by fire, in Jesus name.
17. Father, let every altar or shrine in my village working against my fruitfulness catch fire, in Jesus name
18. Father, let every spirit of money scarcity in the time of need; get out of my life, in Jesus name.
19. Father, let every principality and power closing my door of a miracle, scatter by fire, in Jesus name.
20. Father, let every satanic plantation growing in my life, be uprooted by fire, in Jesus name.

DAY THIRTY- THREE

REMEMBER ME OH LORD

Text: 11Samuel 9:3- 10, 13

Thunder Quote: (if you have not been forgotten, you can't be remembered.)

The disobedience of King Saul altered the kingship position in his lineage, three of his lineage, three of his sons including Jonathan the best friend of David died the same day that Saul died. David decided to show kindness to the family of Saul after the death of Saul according to 11Samuel 9:1,"And David said, Is there yet any that is left of the house of Saul, that I may show him kindness for Jonathan sake?" It was the covenant between David and Jonathan the father of Mephibosheth that starred David up to make such a statement. "That I may show him kindness for Jonathan sake." Covenant is an agreement. Jonathan made an agreement with David before his death. In 1 Samuel 18:3, "Then Jonathan and David made a covenant because he loved him as his own soul."

Mephibosheth was the grandson of Saul, the son of Jonathan, 11Samuel 4:4, "And Jonathan Saul's son had a son that was lame of his feet. He was five years old when the timing came of Saul and Jonathan out of Jezreel, and his nurse took him up and fled, and it came to pass as she made haste to flee and he fell and became lame. And his name was Mephibosheth." Mephibosheth means an idol breaker, he was from a royal family, his grandfather Saul, was the first king in the history of Israel. Mephibosheth was supposed to be a prince in the palace but found himself in Lodebar suffering. Lodebar is a city in Manasseh in Gilead, a forgetful city in like wilderness or desert. Imagine a prince suffering instead of enjoying the benefit of a prince. Ecclesiastes 10:7, says, I have seen servant upon horse and prince walking as a servant upon the earth.

Looking at the case of the prodigal son in Luke 15:11-32, he was the son of a wealthy man but he was a slave in a foreign land. How can I suffer when my father, God, owns the whole world, God forbid? If you discover that you are from a poor background, make sure you pay the price of greatness if you don't want to suffer and also want your children to suffer. What stagnated your ancestor will not stagnate you, in Jesus name.

The Bible says money is a defense and money answereth all things. A good man will leave an inheritance for his children. There are some wealth that lasts from generation to generation. King Solomon was born with a silver spoon; he came and inherited his father's labor. Before Solomon became a king, his father had provided all the necessary building materials he needed, to build Gods sanctuary.

Many of us are suffering today because our parents failed in providing the necessary provision for us. Like the man in 11king 4:1- 7, he died leaving debt as an inheritance for his family. Don't let your children suffer because you suffer. The reason why God needs to remember you is that you have been forgotten. If you have not been forgotten, you can't be remembered. In Genesis 40,

Joseph interpreted a dream for his fellow prisoner, in the prison, he forgot Joseph after his freedom. God created a problem in the palace of Pharaoh, which only Joseph can solve, the one that forgot to remember Joseph, told Pharaoh about Joseph, that he can interpret his dream. I decree in the name of Jesus, anyone you have helped in the past that is doing well and has forgotten you, that person will never have rest of mind until he\she help you, in Jesus name! If you look at the case of Mephibosheth, he was living in Lodebar, a forgetful city before the favor of God singled him out and relocated him to the palace. Your own Lodebar can be that one room apartment that you've been for over ten years. God will relocate you to your own personal house, in Jesus name. I don't know how many years you've been barren, Jobless, sick, unmarried, failed, disappointed. Today, God will attend to your case, in Jesus name. For God to remember you, you must do something extra ordinary that you've never done before.

i. In Mark 10:46-52, blind Bartimaeus cried out violent, before he got the attention of Jesus, he remembered and eventually, his sight was restored.

ii. In 1Chronicles 4:9-10, Jabez got dissatisfied with his condition, as a matter of fact, he became paranoid in respect of his situation. He called on God, and at the end, God remembered him and granted him his request.

iii. In 11Samuel 1:1-20, Hannah's childless case turned her into a fervent and violent prayer champion in Shiloh, in verse13a, "the Bible says, Now Hannah, she spake in her heart: only her lips moved, and her voice was not heard."

If you close your mouth, your door of remembrance will be closed; a closed mouth is a closed destiny. A baby can only communicate with the mother by crying. As you cry violently like Blind Bartimaeus, not minding who is by your side or those mocking you, your prayers will provoke heaven, you will get heaven's attention and be remembered today, in Jesus mighty name.

In Genesis 8:1 and Genesis 9:1, The Bible says, God remembered Noah and God blessed Noah; today God will remember you and bless you, in Jesus name.

PRAYER BOMB

1. Father, I thank you because you have remembered me today, in Jesus name.
2. My Father, my Father, open my book of remembrance before my helper now, in Jesus name.
3. Father, relocate me from the land of forgotten people to the land of successful people, in Jesus name.
4. My Father my Father, let every principality and power contending with my life, receive fire and scatter by fire, in Jesus name.
5. Father Lord, visit me with a visible testimony that will end struggling and suffering in my life, in Jesus name.
6. Father Lord, arise and release all my miracles that the enemy has detained in their territory by fire, in Jesus name.

7. Father Lord, let anyone denying me of my right, have no rest of mind, until I am compensated, in Jesus name.
8. Any man or woman that have vowed that I will not eat the fruit of my labor, fall down and die, in Jesus name.
9. Angel that carry goodness, favor, miracle, contract, and blessing, come to my direction and locate me now, in Jesus name.
10. My Father, let my book of remembrance, be open before my helpers, in Jesus name
11. Father, laminate my destiny with uncommon breakthrough, in Jesus name.
12. Father, I demand all my unpaid wages in the hard of anybody or organization, I have worked for by fire by force, in Jesus name
13. God of signs and wonders, demonstrate your signs and wonders, in my business, marriage, and family, in Jesus name.
14. Father, let every power in the air, land or sea monitoring my destiny, receive thunder from heaven and scatter, in Jesus name
15. Father dismantle every road blocker programmed to cause hindrance against my progress, in Jesus name
16. Father, please don't let my labor in all my endeavors ends in vain, in Jesus name.
17. Oh Lord my God, push me to my land of greatness, in Jesus name.
18. Glory killer in my household, die by fire, in Jesus name.
19. The garment of death over my life, catch fire, in Jesus name.
20. All my caged money be released by fire, in Jesus name.

DAY THIRTY- FOUR

OPEN MY EYES OH LORD

Text: 11 Kings 6:8-18

Thunder Quote: (Mission without vision is television.)

It is a pity that so many people can see physically but spiritually they are blind. Since the spiritual controls the physical, many have eyes, but cannot see, because the devil, the god of this world, had blindfolded many destinies. Great miracle ends up being a mirage. In Judges 16:21, the enemy removed Samson eyes after they have dissolved his source of power and his destiny was finally truncated. In Matthew 6:22a, the Bible says, the light of the body is the eyes." Therefore an eyeless body will operate in total darkness. A closed eye is a closed destiny. When God open your eyes, you will see what others cannot see.

According to our text, in verse sixteen, Elisha said, "they that be with us are more than they that be with them." Because God opened his eyes to see horses and chariots of fire surrounding them, which his servant cannot see. The servant of Elisha was spiritually blind, the moment Elisha prayed in verse 17, of our text, God opened the eyes of his servant and saw the mountain full of horses and chariot of fire round about them. "An adage says, what a boy will stand up and look and cannot see, an adult will sit down and see it clearly." How close you are with God will determine how he will relate to you. If you want to see deep into the spiritual realm, you must be very close to God. In Daniel 2:22, the Bible says, He revealeth the deep and secret things. You need the vision to fulfill your mission on earth. The eye is the organ of vision in a man. It helps in projecting a man's vision. It is also one of the most vital organs in the human body. Without your eyes, you may not get to your destination. Imagine a man without eyes that want to travel from the village to the city to visit a relative. Your eyes give direction to your destiny. A blind man can be easily misled.

If you can see it, you will get it. As long as you can see, it will determine where you will attain. Mission without vision is television. In Gen 21: 14-20, when Abraham sent Hager and her son away, she was wandering in the wilderness, and a time came that they needed water, she lifted up her voice and wept, God heard the voice of the lad, I guess the lad was crying because he was thirsty. In verse 19, the Bible says, and God opened her eyes and she saw a well of water, and she went and filled the bottle with water, and gave the lad to drink. Ishmael would have died of thirst if God had not opened the eye of her mother to see the well. When God opened your eyes, you will see hidden opportunities that ordinary eyes cannot see. God can decide to make man blind just to glorify himself by proving that He can close and open, and can also open and close. The case of the man that was born blind in John 9:1-11, is evidence. What amazed me in the case of this man was, after he got his sight, all eyes were upon him, he became a topic in his neighborhood and people around testified, in verse 32, "Since the world began was it not heard that any man opened the eyes of one that was born blind." Mark 10:46-52, talks about a blind man called Bartimaeus before Jesus opened his eyes, he was crying violently for mercy, despite the crowd surrounding him. You don't need recommended glasses for your spiritual eyes to open, neither do you need to go to an optician or oculist to regain your sight; all you need is JESUS, the eyes opener. Rise up and cry to God violently the way Bartimaeus cried.

PRAYER BOMB

1. Father; I thank you for opening my eyes against any spiritual blindness, in Jesus name.
2. Father, let every Satanic veil covering my eyes from seeing opportunities that will make me great in life, receive fire from the Holy Ghost, in Jesus name.
3. Father, I wash my eyes with the Blood of Jesus against every satanic scale covering my spiritual eyes, in Jesus name.
4. Father, let every enemy from my village, neighborhood or place of work monitoring me about; catch fire now, in Jesus name.
5. Father, let every enemy surrounding my business, marriage, career and my life, go blind and die by fire, in Jesus name.
6. Father open my eyes to see every plan of my enemies, in Jesus name.
7. Father, every register containing people that will never make it in my generation, I remove my name from it, in Jesus name.
8. Father, I speak progress, promotion elevation, and favor into my life today, in Jesus name.
9. My Father my Father, let every link that I have with dead people, break by fire, in Jesus name.

10. Father, let every calabash or container holding my Glory, receive fire and break into pieces, in Jesus name.
11. All evil eyes monitoring my movement, I pluck you out, in Jesus name.
12. Father, let owners of evil loads in my life, carry their loads and die by fire, in Jesus name.
13. Father, let every voice from the grave yard calling my name, be silent forever, in Jesus name.
14. Father, I cut off by the sword of fire, every tongue releasing incantation against my destiny, in Jesus name.
15. Father, every music of sorrow reminding me of my problem, I put a stop to it now, in Jesus name.
16. Power to rule over all my enemies, possess my life, in Jesus name.
17. Father, I revoke every curse of short life against me, by the blood of Jesus.
18. Spirit of long life, come upon me and grant me long life, in Jesus name.
19. Father, let my season of waiting for end today, in Jesus name
20. My Father my Father, open my eyes to see opportunities that will take me to the top today, in Jesus name.

DAY THIRTY- FIVE
MARKED FOR PROMOTION
Text: I Samuel 16:6-13

Thunder Quote: (it is the favor of God that grants a man promotion.)

Divine means coming from God or connected with God. Promotion means advancement in status. It also means to move to a more important Job or rank in a company or an organization.

In the account of our text, when Saul disobeyed God, he was rejected and demoted. God decided to replace him. David was discovered and was promoted from a Shepherd to a king within 24 hours.

Divine promotion means when God:

1. Change your level like Jabez, in 1 Chronicles 4:9-10.
2. Elevate you like Mordecai, in Esther 6:11.
3. Favor you the way He favors Esther, in Esther 3:17-17.
4. Decide to remember you like Mephibosheth, in 11 Samuel 9:1-13.
5. Gives you an open door like Solomon, in 1kings 3:12-13.
6. Open a new chapter in your life, like brother Job, in Job 42:10.
7. Put a new song in your mouth like Hannah, in 1Samuel 1:28.

In Psalm 75:6-7, the scripture says, "For promotion cometh neither from the east, nor from the west, nor from the south, but God is the Judge, he putteth down one, and setteth up another." Also in 1Samuel 2:7-8, "The LORD maketh poor, and maketh rich: he bringeth low, and lifteth up. He raiseth up the poor out of the dust, and lifteth up the beggar from the dunghill, to set them among princes, and to make them inherit the throne of glory." It is the favor of God that grants a man promotion. All those that experience divine promotion in the Bible were first favored. That is why I believe that without divine favor, you can't be promoted. I decree, in the name of Jesus, a divine favor that will bring promotion into your entire life, receive it now, in Jesus name.

In some cases, some people need to be demoted for you to be promoted.

Haman was demoted for Mordecai to be promoted, in Esther 6:10-12.

Saul was demoted for David to be promoted, in 1Sam 16:1, 13-14.

Vashti was demoted for Esther to be promoted, in Esther 2:17.

I decree in the authority name of Jesus, anyone or anybody occupying your seat of promotion, God will demote them today and you will occupy your seat of promotion! Nobody will take your place in your marriage, business, career or ministry, in Jesus name. That seat of promotion that God has reserved for you, will never be taken by another person! You will sit on the seat according to God's timing, in Jesus name.

Jesus says in Luke 19:13, occupy till I come, by the mandate of the TRINITY, you will occupy your position, in Jesus name. Again I say, nobody will ever take your position, in Jesus name. And if there is any man or woman planning your downfall or demotion to replace you, they will fall down and die by fire, in Jesus name. That promotion that you are due for your in your place of work, marriage or ministry will locate you within 24 hours, in Jesus name. 7 days from now, if I am a man of God, anyone delaying your promotion will go on a journey of no return, and you will be promoted, in Jesus name.

I see God stepping into your case, to endorse your promotion Himself, God will arise on your behalf today, in Jesus name! When you are due for a promotion and you are deprived, it only takes divine intervention for your promotion to be released. This month, God will compel anyone in a position to promote you, to promote you with immediate effect, in Jesus name.

Everyone in the scripture that experience promotion has a connection with the source of promotion. Your relationship with the source of promotion will determine your promotion. May the Almighty God place you permanently on your seat of promotion, in Jesus name.

PRAYER BOMB

1. Father, I thank you because today marks the beginning of my promotion in my life, in Jesus name.
2. My Father, my maker, please arise and promote me today, in Jesus name
3. Father, every file that contains the people that will be demoted, I remove my name from it, in Jesus name.
4. Father, let anyone that needs to be demoted for me to be promoted in my place of work, receive sack letter now, in Jesus name.
5. Father, let any man or woman occupying my position in life, give up the ghost, in Jesus name.
6. Anybody, anywhere that wants me to be demoted in order to replace me, your plan will never work; die by fire, in Jesus name.
7. Father, that seat of promotion reserve for me. I occupy by fire, in Jesus name.
8. Father, I decree and prophesy, before the sunset today, I shall be promoted, in Jesus name.
9. My Father in heaven, by-pass every man-made law and endorse my promotion by fire by force, in Jesus name.
10. Father, anyone or anybody in authority that need to approve my promotion, will not have rest of mind until I am promoted, in Jesus name.
11. Father, I need a divine favor that brings promotion before men, in Jesus name.
12. Father, by your garment of divine promotion that is upon my life, give me a rapid promotion in every ramification of life, in Jesus name.

13. My overdue promotion manifest by fire, in Jesus name.
14. Father, let every evil plot and conspiracy to expel me in business, marriage or career, scatter by fire by thunder, in Jesus name
15. My destiny, by the power in the name of Jesus, shine, and keep shining from now henceforth, in Jesus name.
16. Father, let anybody occupying my seat of promotion, fall down and die, in Jesus name.
17. Father, Ordain my promotion so that I will be promoted, in Jesus name.
18. Father, let your original plans for my life, begin to manifest as from today, in Jesus name.
19. Father, let every power of darkness saying no to my progress; receive fire now and give up, in Jesus name.
20. Father, give me a permanently open door of promotion, in every area of my life, in Jesus name.

DAY THIRTY-SIX

IT IS MY TURN TO LAUGH

Text: Genesis 21:1-6

Thunder quote: (life is turned by turn, wait for your turn.)

Life is turned by turn, wait for your own turn. You need to be patient for your turn to come if you don't want to miss your turn. Sarah experienced barrenness for decades, despite the prophecy that she is going to become a mother of nations. Due to barrenness, she decided to allow her husband have sex with her maid Hagar, thinking through that process her own child would come. Hagar conceived, she despised Sarah. And after 14years when Hagar's son Ishmael was born, it became the turn of Sarah. God remembered her, she conceived and gave birth to Isaac and testified in Genesis 21:6 says, "God hath made me laugh so that all that hear will laugh with me." I decree in the name of Jesus, it is your turn to laugh! All those that laughed at you, will soon come and laugh with you, in Jesus name.

The laugh is an expression of joy. Laugh means, to make the sound and movement of your face that shows you are happy or think something is funny. It also means, when you are in the very good position because you have done something successful. Laugh can manifest in the following below:

i. When you have just been promoted in your office from a marketer to the managing director, you will laugh.
ii. They just endorsed your visa with 4 years stay after 7 years of applying, you will laugh.
iii. A week after your landlord gave you quite notice; a friend gave you a flat in lekki in your name with C of O. You will laugh.
iv. Someone you know that was barren for over 35years and has passed the age of menopause just had a triplet, you will laugh.
v. A friend of yours that was given death sentence in the court, his case was reverse miraculously, you will laugh.

May be it has been long you laugh, before sunrise tomorrow; God will give you a breakthrough, that will cause you to laugh, in Jesus name. There is someone reading this book, your laughter will bring confusion to your enemies, they will think you are mad, not knowing that what they thought was impossible, God had made it possible. Luke 6:21 says, "Blessed are yet that weep now, for ye shall laugh." By the mandate of the Trinity, your season of weeping has ended! Welcome to your season of laughter, in Jesus name. In Psalm 30:5, the Bible says, "Weeping may endure for a night but joy cometh in the morning." I don't know how long you have been weeping in the secret, from today; it will end, in Jesus name. That particular problem in your home, family or business that you don't even understand how it started, very soon, you will laugh over it, in Jesus name. There is a time to laugh-Ecclesiastes 3:4. Again I say to the reader of this book, welcome to your season of laughter, in Jesus name. As from today, the tears that will come out of your eyes will be tears of joy, in the mighty name of Jesus. Job 8:21 says, "Till he fills thy mouth with laughing and your lips with rejoicing."

God will add laughter with every word that comes out of your mouth. God says He will laugh at anyone laughing at you in Psalm 37:12. Hannah was a woman that experienced shame in her matrimonial home due to barrenness in 1Samuel 1:6, "And her adversary also provoked her sore for to make fret, because the LORD had shut up her womb." The second wife of her husband mocked her often and finally, in verse 19 of the same chapter, God remembered her. God will remember you today and end every mockery situation in your life, in Jesus name.

The moment the first son of Hannah was born, it silent the voice of Peninah that was laughing at her, and at the end, Hannah became a mother of children. I pray for you, by the power, in the name of Jesus, the miracle that will silent everybody mocking you, in your marriage, career, and business; receive it now, in Jesus name. I remember some years before I got married, I traveled to my village for the New Year festival, one of my friends, embarrassed me in the public saying, when will my daughter stop calling you brother? I wasn't happy with me, I said God you've heard him, the following year, I came to the same village with my wife. That shame and reproach in your life have been consumed by fire, in Jesus name. In verse six of our text, in Genesis twenty-one, Sarah concluded that "God hath made me laugh so that all that hear will laugh with me." I decree upon your life before you finish reading this book, God will give you a miracle that will make you laugh and when people hear your testimony, they will come and laugh with you, in Jesus name. Don't worry, be happy!

PRAYER BOMB

1) Father, I thank you for making it my turn to laugh, in Jesus name.
2) Father, every mouth that is mocking me, shut it up permanently for my sake, in Jesus name.
3) My Father my creator, turn every weeping in my life to joy, in Jesus name.
4) Oh Lord my God, every problem in my life that I cannot relate to anybody, I hand it over to you, in Jesus name.
5) Father, let every suffering and smiling situation, end in my life now, in Jesus name.
6) Father, every memory of shame in my life, wipe it off, in Jesus name.
7) Father, let anyone or anybody, reminding me of my problems so that I will be sorrowful, be disgraced with shame, in Jesus name.
8) Father, every music of sorrow, shame and reproach the enemy is using to entertain me; I put it off, in Jesus name.
9) Father, it is my turn to laugh, make me laugh, in Jesus name.
10) God of Elijah, arise by fire and consume every problem in my life that is making people ask where my God is, in Jesus name.
11) Father, before the end of today, gives me a testimony that will make me laugh, in Jesus name.
12) Father, everyone that laugh at me yesterday, give me a breakthrough today, that will cause them to come and laugh with me, in Jesus name.
13) Father, connect me to the source of miracles so that my life will be meaningful, in Jesus name.

14) Father, roll away by fire, every reproach upon my destiny, in Jesus name.
15) Father, perfume my life with the aroma of favor, in Jesus name.
16) My Father my Father, turn every challenge in my life into a stepping stone to my breakthrough, in Jesus name.
17) Father Lord, put a stop to anything that wants to stop me from laughing, in Jesus name.
18) Father, let every evil spirit from the pit of hell monitoring my miracle; receive fire and scatter, in Jesus name.
19) Father, the joy I have started this year with, it will not end with sorrow, in Jesus name.
20) God of Isaac, because you are the God of laughter, don't let me ever weep again, in Jesus name.

DAY THIRTY- SEVEN

THE PRESENT HELPER IN THE TIME OF NEEDS

Text: 1kings 17:8-16

Thunder Quote: (The help that comes from above is above all.)

There is nobody on the earth that doesn't need help, some have god-fathers that they run to when in need, some also have God the Father that they run to when any needs arise. There is different between help from abroad and help from above. Help from abroad is limited, while help from above is unlimited. When God help you, men will be willing to help you. In Psalm46:1, the Bible says, "God is our refuge and strength, a very present help in trouble." The only person you can call when in trouble that can help you at any moment is God, which is the reason why He is called the present helper. Vain is the help of man. The same man tells you, I will help you can fail. I pray for you today, anybody that has promised to help you, will help you, in Jesus name! That your destiny helper will locate you, before sunrise tomorrow! In the account of Psalm 121:2, David said, "My help cometh from the LORD, which made heaven and earth." The help that comes from above is above all. I decree in the name of Jesus, before you finish reading this book, help you never bargain for will locate you, in Jesus name! God will give your life a meaning by opening a new chapter of glory in your life and give you a new song, in Jesus name.

HOW TO OBTAIN HELP IN THE TIME OF NEED

Using the story of the widow of Zarephath, in 1King 17:8-16. Let consider some ways to obtain help in the time of needs.

1. Diligent: She was gathering fire wood when the man of God came to meet her. Proverbs 22:29, "seest thou a man diligent in his business? He shall stand before kings; he shall not stand before mean men." She was not sitting at home idle. God can never help a lazy man. Hard work is part of life, you must work hard.

2. Obedient: In verse 10 and 11 of our text, in the Bible says, "fetch me I pray the little water in the vessel, that I may drink, and as she was going to fetch it, he called to her and said bring me, I pray thee a morsel of bread in thine hand." Imagine somebody that is not her husband commanding her to entertain him, some women in her condition will insult anybody that tries such a thing, even some married woman will never take such a thing. She obeyed 100 percent, verse 15 says, and she went and did according to the saying of Elijah and she and her child did eat for many days. Total obedient brings complete blessing. In Isaiah 1:19, the Bible says, "if ye will be willing and obedient ye shall eat the good of the land." Obedient is better than sacrifice.

3. Be Honest: According to verse 12, And she said, as the Lord thy God liveth, I have not a cake, but a handful of meal in a barrel. Integrity brings favor and uncommon blessing. Success without integrity never last.

4. Avoid Excuse: Excuse only delay and deny one of her miracles, don't allow your problem to tell you. If you allow your condition to hinder you from taking the risk, that will take you to the top, you will remain at the bottom. Don't ever give an excuse.

5. Apply Faith: Verse 13 says, and Elijah said unto her, fear not. Her faith made her obey the man of God completely, and verse 15, Bible says, she went and did according to the saying of Elijah. In 11Chronicles 20:20, the Bible says, "Belief in the Lord your God, so shall ye be established, believe his prophets, so shall ye prosper."

6. Give to Men of God: The Bible says, there is a reward attached to people who give to servants of God. When you give to a man of God and he blesses you, heaven will endorse it. Givers never lack. The gift of a man maketh room for him and bringeth him before great men, Proverbs 18:16. Because she gave, what she gave was given back to her in abundance. She has excess food in her house that sustained her and her son for three and half years. When you give to a man of God, you will receive a heavenly reward.

7. Look unto God for Help: In Psalm 121:1-2, David said, his help only cometh from God. Let your focus be on your source, the Almighty God. Philippians 4:19 says, My God, shall supply all my need according to His riches in glory by Christ Jesus. Also in John 3:27, the Bible says, a man can receive nothing except it be given him from heaven. If you need help in the time of needs rise up as you access heaven violently.

PRAYER BOMB

1. Father, I thank you because you are my present help in the time of needs, in Jesus name.
2. Father Lord, please I need help from above, abroad and within, in Jesus name.
3. My Father, my Father, suspend everything you are doing now, and help me, in Jesus name.
4. My Father, every secret sin in my life, standing as a hindrance to my breakthrough, Lord deliver me and have mercy on me, in Jesus name.
5. Father, please send help to me in time of needs, in Jesus name.
6. Father, let anyone or anybody assigned to help me in life, locate me now, in Jesus name.
7. My Father, my Father, because you are the present help, please help me to prosper in life, in Jesus name.
8. Father Lord, I command the east wind, west wind, north wind, and south wind, to blow favor to my direction now, in Jesus name.
9. Father Lord, every fire of the enemy burning in my life, Holy Ghost fire, put it off, in Jesus name.
10. Father Lord, let the helper I have been expecting arrive, in Jesus name.
11. Father Lord, give me victory over every current problem disgracing me before my fellow human-being, in Jesus name.
12. Father, let every demon chasing help away from me; receive fire and scatter, in Jesus name.
13. Father Lord, from the four corners of this world, send help to me now, in Jesus name.

14. Father Lord, send my destiny helpers to me, to begin to help me from today, in Jesus name.
15. Father Lord, put my helpers in a strategic position where they will help me, in Jesus name.
16. Father Lord, because you are the helper of the helpless, please deliver me from every hopeless situation, in Jesus name.
17. Father Lord, position me on the top so that I will never go down, in Jesus name.
18. Father, let every ugly situation in my life, that is bringing mockery to your name; receive fire, in Jesus name.
19. Father Lord, connect me back to the socket of testimony so that I will be testifying again, in Jesus name.
20. Father, give me a breakthrough, that will turn me into a topic in the world, in Jesus name.

DAY THIRTY-EIGHT

I WILL NOT LABOR IN VAIN

Text: Joshua 16:11-13

Thunder Quote: (if you are empty within, you will be defeated.)

Nobody likes to labor without being paid or compensated at the end. In all labor, there is profit according to proverbs 14:23a. The case of Caleb was likened to one of the versatile, strong, committed, faithful, bold, rugged, determined, zealous and trained soldier, that was given an assignment by the government of it country, to rescue some citizens in the hand of the terrorist group, and after rescuing the citizens he was not compensated, or the case of some USA war expertise assign to capture one of the most notorious terrorists Usama-Bin Ladin, imagine after taking the risk and mission completed, they were not rewarded.

How will you feel, if you are the person that brought victory, and you were forgotten? In Numbers 13:32-33, God instructed Moses to send twelve men to go and spy the land of Canaan, the promise-land, ten out of the twelve can back with the evil report about the land, only Caleb and Joshua brought a good report about the land they went to spy. In Numbers 13:13-33, the fearful men responded, "We be not able to go against the people, for they are stronger than we.

The inhabitant thereof and all the people that we saw in it are men of great status. And there we saw the giants, the son of Anak which come of the people that we were in our own sight as grasshoppers, and so we were in their sight." As a man thinketh in his heart so he is, Proverb 23:7a. Ten out of the spies saw the inhabitants as giants, and two saw them as ants. How you see challenges of life, matters a lot. Some people see their problem as a mountain, other see theirs as a valley. In Numbers 13:30, the Bible says, "And Caleb stilled the people before Moses, and said, let us go up at once, and possess it: for we are well able to overcome it." It takes boldness and courage to confront giants. The wicked flee when no man pursueth: but the righteous are as bold a lion-Proverbs 28:1. If you are empty within, you will be defeated. Caleb was bold because of what he carries. The Bible confirms it in Numbers 14:24, that there is another spirit in Caleb. In 1John 4:4b, the Bible says, "Greater is he that is in you, than he that is in the world." When you carry God, you carry a greater power and lesser power must bow. By the power in the name of JESUS, every principality and power contending with your destiny are destroyed!

After Caleb had risked his life by going to spy the land of Canaan, he demanded, his own allocation of land since Moses that sent him is late, and Joshua his successor, has started allocating land to people. Wherever you have labored and you have not been paid, may God arise for you now and release all your entitlement to you, in Jesus name. In most of our military barracks, we have many widows suffering, who lost their husbands in the process of fighting for the nation. Some of them went on peace keeping missions in other countries and died in the process, and they their family have not been settled. Also, there is so many retired armed forces personnel, who have not been given entitlements or pensions. A lot of service men have died as a result of thinking of-payment of their pensions or gratuities. Some of the unpaid individuals will say, after all my labor, and suffering, there is nothing to show forth, as a result of this, they died. I pray for you reading this book; God will intervene on your behalf and in any area anyone owes you, you will be paid, in Jesus name. In 1Peter 5:10, the Bible says, "But the God of all grace, who hath called us unto his eternal glory by Christ Jesus, after that ye have suffered a while, make you perfect, establish, strengthen, and settle you." I prophesy into your entire life, you will not labor in vain, in every area of your life, in Jesus name. When you are steadfast, unmovable and always abounding in the work of the Lord, your labor won't be in vain-1Corinthians 15:58. God is not unrighteous to forget your good work and labor of love, according to Hebrew 6:10. 11Timothy 2:6 says, "The husbandman that laboureth must be first partaker of the fruits." I have no doubt, that concerning you reading this book, all your entitlements that you have been denied off, all these years will be given back to you without any delay, in Jesus name. In Genesis 29; Jacob served his uncle for seven years because of Rachel that he loved, his uncle Laban deprived him of his right. Jacob said to his uncle Laban in Genesis 29:21"Give me my wife, for my days, are fulfilled, that I may go in unto her." I pray for you once more, anyone or anybody denying you of your right, God will trouble him or her to give you what belongs to you, in Jesus name!

Joseph interpreted a dream for his co-prisoner in the prison, and he told him that after his release, he should remember him, but the butler forgot him- Genesis 40:14, 23. Have you helped somebody, and you have been forgotten, God will create a problem that will him to remember you again, in Jesus name. That man you have labored with in marriage will not leave you for another woman!

That organization that you have saved from the hand of fraudster that sacked you will look for you again, in Jesus name!

In Esther 6, Mordecai helped a particular king from the hands of some people that planned a coup against the king, he was remembered at last. May God open the book of remembrance for you before your helpers, in Jesus name!

PRAYER BOMB

1. Father, I thank you because I will not labor in vain, in my business, marriage, and career, in Jesus name.
2. Every territorial enemy terrorizing my life, business, and marriage, receive fire and die by fire, in Jesus name.
3. Every spirit of laboring without any result to show forth operating in my life, get out of my life, in Jesus name.
4. Every arrow of regret fired into my destiny, come out by fire and back fire to the sender, in Jesus name.
5. Every force of darkness forcing me not to achieve a result in life, receive fire and scatter by fire, in Jesus name.
6. Heaven of miracles, favor, and breakthroughs, open upon my life, in Jesus name
7. My Father my Father, let every principality and power contending with my life receive fire and scatter by fire, in Jesus name.
8. Father, visit me with visible testimonies that will end struggling and suffering in my life, in Jesus name.
9. Father, arise and release my entire miracles that the enemies have detained in their territories by fire, in Jesus name.

10. Father, anyone denying me of my right, will not have rest of mind, until I am compensated, in Jesus name.
11. Father, any man or woman that has vowed that I will not eat the fruit of my labor, shall fall down and die, in Jesus name
12. Angel that carry goodness, favor, miracles, contracts, and blessing, come to my direction now, in Jesus name.
13. Father, let my book of remembrance, be open before my helper, in Jesus name.
14. My Father, my Father, I have suffered enough in this life, please intervene and turn my life around, in Jesus name.
15. Father, laminate my destiny with uncommon breakthrough, in Jesus name.
16. Father, I demand all my unpaid wages in the hands of anybody or organization, I have worked for by fire by force, in Jesus name.
17. God of signs and wonders, demonstrate your signs and wonders in my business, marriage, and family, in Jesus name.
18. Father, let every power in the air, land or sea monitoring my destiny; receive thunder from heaven and scatter, in Jesus name.
19. Father, dismantle every road blocker programmed to cause hindrance against my progress, in Jesus name.
20. Father, please don't let my labor in my entire endeavors end in vain, in Jesus name.

DAY THIRTY-NINE
OPEN A NEW CHAPTER IN MY LIFE
Text: 1Samuel 16:11-13

Thunder Quote: (When God open a new chapter in your life, your old chapter will close.)

David was in the old chapter of his life as a shepherd, the moment God opened a new chapter in his life, he experienced uncommon promotion that turned him into a king under 24 hours. A new chapter is also a new beginning. The reason why God needs to open a new chapter in your life is that you have dwelt long on the old chapter. 11Corinthians 5:17 says, "If a man is in Christ, He is a new creature, old thing are passed away, behold all things become new." it is your covenant right as a bonafide child of God to experience new things, in every ramification of your life.

God says you are a new creature, that is, you are a no more ordinary person, you have been transformed to an extraordinary person and everything about you will become new. When God opens a new chapter in your life, your old chapter will close. In 11kings 5, a man called Naaman, who was a captain in the military, suffered a killer disease called Leprosy, he had an encounter with Prophet Elisha, he was asked to go and dip himself seven times in the river for healing, he reluctantly complied, and after the exercise, his flesh came again like unto the flesh of a little child.

Leprosy became an old chapter in the life of Naaman, for God to open a new chapter in his life; God had to go into his past, reverse it, and gave him a brand new flesh. In Jeremiah 32:27, God says, Behold, I am the LORD, the God of all flesh: Is there anything too hard for me? If with God all things are possible, then, your own case will not be difficult for God to handle. A man was in his own car when he saw his neighbor trying to enter a public transport, what came out of his mouth was, "I know you will never stop entering public transport." God heard it, before sunset that very day, his neighbor that he abused came back home with a brand new car. It is only God that has the final say over your life, whose report will you believe, man or God? The Bible says, let God be true and let all men be a liar, and God is not a man that should lie. He says in his word, in Jeremiah 29:11, "That his thoughts toward you are thought of peace." He decides on his own, nobody can question him. If he decides to remove the old chapters like; failure, poverty, shame, barrenness, sickness, curses and bring the new chapters like success, prosperity, glory, fruitfulness, good health, and blessing, nobody can question him. I decree in the name that is above all other names, May God delete the old chapter in your life and open a new chapter in your life, in Jesus name! Your era of a new beginning has commenced now, in Jesus name!

In Isaiah 43:18-19, the Bible says, Remember ye, not the former things, neither consider the things of old, behold I will do a new thing: now it shall spring forth; shall ye not know it? I will even make a way in the wilderness and rivers in the desert". God is only interested in doing new things, and I see him doing new things in your life with effect from now, in Jesus name!

WHAT HAPPEN WHEN GOD OPENS A NEW CHAPTER FOR YOU

1. All eyes will be on you: John 9:1-7, talks about a man that was blind from his birth, after Jesus restored back his sight in verse 8:9, the neighbors which before had seen him that he was blind said, is not this he that sat and begged? Some said, this is he, others said, he is like him, but he said, I am he. As for you reading this book before the sun rises tomorrow, the miracle that will make people focus on you, receive it now, in Jesus name!

2. You will turn to the topic of discussion in your society: The same man in John 9:1-7, because his miracle was an amazing one, he became news and a topic in the society that particular day, people came to find out how he received his miracle.

3. Your level will change: David was just an ordinary Shepherd boy before he was made a king; Joseph was also a slave boy before he became a prime minister in Egypt.

4. Favor will locate you: In the book of Esther, if you read clearly, you will discover that Esther was not even qualified to be a queen in a strange land but the favor of God demoted the formal queen for her to become the new queen- Esther 2:17.

5. Things will begin to work well for you: Things begins to work well for Jabez when God opened a new chapter in his life. 1Chronicles 4:9-10.

PRAYER BOMB

1. Father, I thank you for opening a new chapter in every area of my life, in Jesus name.
2. Father, position me on the right part, to the road of success, in Jesus name.
3. Father, don't let my own case be difficult for you to solve, in Jesus name.
4. Father, rewrite the story of my life with a new beginning of a new testimony, breakthrough and miracle, in Jesus name.
5. Father, open a new chapter in my life and give me a new song in Jesus name.
6. Father, elevate me from zero level to hero level, in Jesus name.
7. Father Lord, every old chapter of failure, poverty, and shame in my life, close it now, in Jesus name.
8. Father, reflect your glory in my life so that my life will have to mean, in Jesus name.
9. Father, let any satanic priest contacted by anybody to alter my destiny, fall down and die, in Jesus name
10. Father, catapult my business, marriage, and finance to the mountain of miracles, in Jesus name.
11. Father, I regain back my original position that the enemy had taken from me, in Jesus name.
12. Father, restore back all my wasted years the enemy had eaten, in Jesus name.
13. My destiny, hear the word of the Lord, receive the light of God and shine brighter than ever before, in Jesus name.
14. Father, let your original plan and purpose concerning me, come to reality, in Jesus name.

15. Father, let every power from my father's house contending with my destiny, become powerless, in Jesus name.
16. My Father my Father, let every destiny stopper arranged from the pit of hell, to stop my progress in life, die by fire, in Jesus name.
17. Father Lord, every past mistake in my life, that is robbing me of my covenant right, lord have mercy on me, in Jesus name.
18. My Father, my Father, before I leave this world, people will hear good things about me, in Jesus name.
19. Father Lord, give me a testimony, which will turn me into a topic of discussion, in my family Jesus name.
20. My Father, my Father, do something new in my life, which will turn my destiny around for good, in Jesus name.

DAY FORTY

BALANCE YOUR MIRACLES WITH THANKSGIVING

Text: Luke 17:11-19

Thunder Quote: (when you thank God, your tank of miracles will over flow.)

Thanksgiving means, the expression of gratitude to God or to show gratitude to somebody, that you appreciate the good thing, he/she has done for you. Many of us want God to do something new for us but failed to thank him for the ones He has done. It is only the grateful that can thank God. If you are not grateful, you can't be great. The ungrateful will always find it very difficult to thank God. When you thank God, your tank of miracles will overflow.

Thanksgiving is a way of telling God to do more for you. The more you thank God, the more you are compelling him to do extra. It is only a fool that will say that there is nothing to thank God for. In lamentation 3:22, the Bible says, "it is of the LORD'S mercies that we are not consumed because his compassion fails not". There is a reason why God spared your life because you are not better than those that are dead. Psalm 124:2-3 also says, "If it had not been the LORD, who was on our side when men rose up against us: Then they had swallowed us when their wrath was kindled against us." In verse eight the Bible concluded, "Our help is in the name of the Lord, who made heaven and earth." Some people hardly see any need to thank God when they have one, or more pending request.

However it is not all that sleep that wakes up to see another day, and it is not all that goes out, that return back. The fact that you are still alive is a major reason why you must give thanks to God. Some of us don't even thank God for saving our souls because the majority of us are heading to hell before Jesus saved us. There are unseen battles he fought and won on our behalf. You can also thank God in advance; if you thank Him in advance, it will propel Him to bring your desire to reality on time.

Imagine a tenant that is still under a landlord, thanking God for making him a landlord, or a fifty-nine years old barren woman, thanking God for making her a mother of children. It may look foolish and impossible, but Thanksgiving can stir God to give someone a unmerited favor. It is our duties as children of God to thank God. 1Thessalonians 5:18 says, "In everything give thanks: for this is the will of God in Christ Jesus concerning you."Thanksgiving is the master key to gain access into the gate of God. Psalm 100:4 says, "Enter into his gates with thanksgiving and into his court with praises: be thankful unto him, and bless his name." The gates are in plural form, it can be the gate of miracle, favor, promotion, breakthrough, success, blessing, good health, prosperity and promotion. When you add thanksgiving to praise, it grants you quick access to God's master bedroom.

Back to our text, ten lepers came to Jesus to be healed of their leprosy. Ten of them came and they were all healed; but only one of them was made whole because he came back to thank God, after receiving his miracle. To be healed and to be made whole is not the same. When you are healed you become healthy again, but when you are made whole, it means you are completely healed. I pray for you in the name of Jesus, your miracle will be completed before this spiritual exercise, and you will have a reason to give God thanks, in Jesus name!

PROFITS OF THANKSGIVING

1. Thanksgiving is like an invitation to God.
2. It opens doors to a greater miracle.
3. It seals and makes your miracle permanent.
4. It is an open cheque to God's treasures.
5. It can reverse the irreversible.
6. It brings to remembrance before God your quality service.
7. It can change impossibility to possibility.
8. It preserves your miracles.

PRAYER BOMB

1. Father, I thank you for the grace to be thankful to you, for everything you have done for me, in Jesus name.
2. Father Lord, give me a grateful and thankful heart, in Jesus name.
3. Father Lord, as long as I am still alive, always give me a reason to thanks, in Jesus name.

4. Father Lord, as I begin to appreciate you, give me a complete miracle, so that, there will be turn around in my entire life, in Jesus name.
5. Father, give me extra testimonies that will advertise your name more in my life, in Jesus name.
6. Father Lord, as I begin to appreciate you, overshadows my destiny with divine favor, which will elevate me to a greater height in life, in Jesus name.
7. My Father, my Father, as I begin to appreciate you, let my gate of miracle, favor promotion, connection, success and prosperity, open by fire, in Jesus name.
8. Father Lord, as I appreciate you, perfume my destiny with testimonies, which will overcome every problem, reigning in my life, in Jesus name.
9. Father Lord, as I appreciate you, scatter by fire every satanic strongly mounted to attack my business, marriage, family, and career, in Jesus name.
10. Father Lord, as I appreciate you, let every spirit ingrate in my life, hindering you, from doing new things in my life, come out by fire, in Jesus name.
11. Father Lord, by the reason of the covenant that I have with the blood of the lamb. As I appreciate you, let every evil covenant against my destiny break by fire, in Jesus name.
12. Father Lord, balance the equation of my entire life with testimonies so that my life will become meaningful, in Jesus name
13. Father Lord, as I appreciate you, uproot by fire, every satanic weed growing in my life, in Jesus name.

14. Father Lord, as I appreciate you, fertilize my destiny with the oil of divine promotion which brings rapid promotion, in Jesus name.
15. Father Lord, as I appreciate you, reverse every irreversible curse upon my destiny to blessing, in Jesus name.
16. My Father my Father, as I appreciate you, end every long time battle and war in my life, in Jesus name.
17. Father Lord, as I appreciate you, destroy every spirit of leprosy upon my life, in Jesus name.
18. Father Lord, every satanic boundary or line of limitation against my destiny, I cross over it, in Jesus name.
19. Father Lord, as I appreciate you, let every river of poverty surrounding my business, marriage, family, and finance, dry up by fire, in Jesus name.
20. My Father, my Father, as I appreciate you, let your mercy answer me, in Jesus name.

ABOUT THE BOOK

PRAYER WORKS is forty days and forty nights prayer plan, specially prepared for your spiritual explosion and breakthroughs in life.

In Luke 4:1-14, Our Lord Jesus Christ discovered the importance of forty days and 40 nights, before he commenced his ministry. He spent his own forty days and forty nights in the wilderness, a wild region that is very difficult to live. In verse 14, the Bible says, "And Jesus returned in the power of the spirit into Galilee and there went out a fame of him through the entire region about him. "If you close your mouth, your door of remembrance will be closed; a closed mouth is a closed destiny. A baby can only communicate with the mother by crying. Cry aloud to God and He will answer you! These prayers will work for you, in Jesus mighty name!

ABOUT THE AUTHOR

Olusegun Festus Remilekun also was known as Pastor Fessy, is an evangelist, public speaker and a vessel of honor in the hands of God.

He is currently the president of Prophetic Declaration Ministries, also known as Prayerland Harvest Ministries International, an organization devoted to reaching the four corners of the world with the Gospel of Jesus Christ, bringing succor to the less privileged in the society, and setting people who are bound free from the shackles of Satan through the power of prophetic prayers and preaching the word of God.

He operates in power, teaching, and pastoral ministry. He is available for counseling, prayers, preaching and also for seminars. He is the author of best sellers' book-Prophetic Declarations for Breakthroughs.

Olusegun is married to Grace and they are blessed with children.

OTHER BOOKS BY THE AUTHOR

1. Prophetic Declarations for Breakthroughs (Volume 1) 35, Powerful Life Changing Declarations for Daily Breakthroughs.
2. Holy Ghost Night
3. Every day with Jesus
4. Use of Psalms for Mercy, Justice, Help, Success, and Favor of God
5. 777 Dreams and Prophetic Interpretations
6. 1001 Prayers to unseat long standing Problems
7. 1250 Golden Promises of God in the Bible for you
8. Family Liberation Prayers
9. Financial Rainfall
10. Overcoming forces of household wickedness
11. 500 Prophetic Night Prayers

Made in the USA
Columbia, SC
19 June 2025